D0894290

UNIVERSITY OF WINNIPEG
LIBRARY
515 Portage Avenue
Winnipeg, Manitoba R3B 2E9

THE JOURNAL OF JACOB FOWLER

F
592
.F78
1970

THE JOURNAL OF JACOB FOWLER

Edited, with notes, by
ELLIOTT COUES

With a preface and additional notes by
RAYMOND W. AND MARY LUND SETTLE
AND HARRY R. STEVENS

Jacob Fowler

UNIVERSITY OF NEBRASKA PRESS · LINCOLN

Publishers on the Plains

UNP

Copyright © 1970 by the University of Nebraska Press

All Rights Reserved

International Standard Book Number 0–8032–0756–5

Library of Congress Catalog Card Number 77–110152

MANUFACTURED IN THE UNITED STATES OF AMERICA

Contents

Preface

The Jacob Fowler journal is one of the most valuable narratives about early travel and exploration in the Southwest. A frontiersman and trader, Fowler kept his journal while on a trading expedition into the area in 1821–22. Fortunately, the original, which he wrote by the light of the campfire when the day's travel or work was done, has escaped the hazards of almost a century and a half and today rests secure in the library of the University of Chicago.

In several respects this journal stands in a class by itself. It was the first complete narrative of an expedition into the little-known Southwest after that of Zebulon Montgomery Pike in 1806–07. In contrast to Pike's journal and other early narratives concerning that part of the country, some of which were official government reports, that of Fowler, who was under no obligation to give his material to the public, was strictly private and personal. He does not state his purpose in keeping a daily record of events. Certainly it was not to promote a literary career or to impart information, for upon his return to Cincinnati in 1822 he placed the journal in his family archives and seems to have been satisfied with the knowledge that only his closest relatives knew of its existence. It remained undisturbed for three generations—too precious to destroy but impossible to read—until in 1898 it was brought to light, transcribed, and edited by Elliott Coues. At that time a small edition, 950 copies, was printed.

Perhaps the first thing the reader notices about this unique document is the author's fantastic and sometimes frustrating misspelling of everyday words. Although he was a literate and knowledgeable man, Fowler used an amazing phonetic system of his own. This was neither strange nor unusual, for in his day schooling and education on the frontier, where he was reared and lived most of his life, was hard to come by even under the best of conditions. Many men, including the most successful, were not very concerned about correct spelling and proper grammar. It should be remembered in Fowler's favor that he was a rugged, intrepid frontiersman of the type of Daniel Boone, Simon Kenton, and Lewis Wetzel—men who stood at the head of the class where deeds of valor and stark courage were concerned but cheerfully passed to the foot when literary accomplishments were in order.

No editorial work whatsoever, such as the correction of spelling, punctuation, or capitalization, has been done on the journal itself; it is a verbatim reprinting of the Coues edition of 1898. As the reader will observe, Elliott Coues's highly valuable footnotes are retained in their entirety. In the original they were numbered only to 99 (number 94 appearing twice in the text) and then began again with 1. Here the footnotes have been renumbered in accordance with the needs of the new edition and are consecutive throughout. New annotation is enclosed within brackets. Cross-references in the Coues notes have been changed to refer to the new pages or footnote numbers. A new index has been prepared and a bibliography has been added. An illustration of Fowler's handwriting included in the Coues edition and the original half-title have been omitted.

The making of a book like this involved vastly more work than that of the editors whose names are attached to it. Many wonderful people whose only motive was to assist in a worthwhile undertaking contributed generously of their time, effort, and inspiring interest. Though the names of all of them cannot be included at this time, their invaluable contributions are hereby acknowledged. Among those whose assistance was of special significance are Dorothy Williams, Librarian, Oklahoma Historical Society; Robert H. Land, Acting Chief of the General Reference and Bibliography Division, Library of Congress, Washington, D.C.; Ethel Hutchins, Head of the Literature Department, Cincinnati and Hamilton County Public Library; Mabel E. Deutrich, Archivist in Charge, Early Wars Branch, General Services Administration, National Archives and Records Service; Lois Jones, Arkansas History Commission; Mrs. Alys Freeze, Head of the Western History Department, Denver Public Library; Charles Van Ravenswaay, Director, Barbara Kell,

Librarian, and Dorothy Brockhoff, Reference Librarian, Missouri Historical Society; Caroline Dunn, Librarian, William Henry Smith Memorial Library, Indiana Historical Society; David C. Mearns, Chief, Manuscripts Division, Library of Congress; Elizabeth C. Hall, Librarian, New York Botanical Garden; Kathryn Johnson, Minnesota Historical Society; Elizabeth McPherson, Manuscripts Division, Library of Congress; Dorothy Milne, Librarian, Monte Vista (Colorado) Public Library; Roland Baughman and Alice H. Bonnell, Columbia University, New York; John D. Stark, Temple University, Philadelphia; Mrs. Alice P. Hook, formerly librarian of the Cincinnati Historical Society; Phyllis Dunham, Librarian, Adams State College, Alamosa, Colorado; Detroit Public Library; Ohio Historical Society; and Richard G. Wood, Chief, Army Section, War Records Branch, National Archives. Others who rendered special service were Judge Allen B. Glenn, Hugh Gibson Glenn, and George Allen Glenn, of Harrisonville, Missouri; Mrs. Arthur R. Evans, Safford, Arizona; Amelia C. McKoun, Bunker Hill, West Virginia; Mrs. Harley L. Griffith, Martinsburg, West Virginia; Emmet F. Horine, Brooks, Kentucky; Helen M. Visnovsky, Johnstown, Pennsylvania; Anna Mary Henshaw, Inwood, West Virginia; and Robert L. Harris, Belmont, California.

Raymond W. and Mary Lund Settle and Harry R. Stevens

The Journal
of
Jacob Fowler

Narrating an Adventure
from
Arkansas through the Indian Territory,
Oklahoma, Kansas, Colorado,
and New Mexico,
to the
Sources of Rio Grande Del Norte,
1821–22

Edited, with notes
by
Elliott Coues

DEDICATED
TO
REUBEN T. DURRETT, A.M., LL.D.,
NESTOR OF KENTUCKY HISTORIANS
AND
PRESIDENT OF THE FILSON CLUB,
IN ADMIRATION OF HIS PERSONAL CHARACTER AND IN
REMEMBRANCE OF PLEASANT HOURS PASSED
IN HIS HOSPITABLE HOME

Introduction

Jacob Fowler is an unknown author whose work has never before been heralded beyond the private circles of his friends, relatives, and descendants. The editor of his Journal has therefore a man as well as a book to introduce to the public. Being responsible for the appearance of the latter in print, he will presently say something on that score. But first let us hear from Colonel R. T. Durrett, of Louisville, Ky., the owner of the manuscript now published, who will speak for its author:

LOUISVILLE, KY., *Dec.* 4, 1897.

DR. ELLIOTT COUES, *Washington, D. C.*

I have your letter, My Dear Doctor, in which you request me to tell what I may know about the Journal you found among my manuscripts when you were my guest last year, and which you have determined to include in your admirable series of Western Americana. I am sorry to have to say that I do not know much of this manuscript or its author. The little I know, however, will be cheerfully contributed to an undertaking which is to place a Kentucky manuscript from my collection among the publications which, under your editorship, have added so much to our literature of discovery, exploration, and adventure.

The author of this Journal is Major Jacob Fowler. His name is not attached to the Journal, and does not appear on any of its pages in such a way as to indicate authorship. Yet it is well understood among his numerous descendants now living in Kentucky and other States that he is the author. I obtained the manuscript some years ago from Mrs. Ida Symmes Coates, daughter of the late Americus

Symmes, now residing at her country seat near Louisville. Mrs. Coates is a great-granddaughter, on the maternal side, of Jacob Fowler. The manuscript descended to her in a direct line from her mother, Frances Scott, who was a granddaughter of Jacob Fowler, and who had obtained it in the same way from her mother, Abigail Fowler, the only daughter of Jacob Fowler. The manuscript has thus come down to us in a direct line, and is the unquestionable work of Major Jacob Fowler.

When Mrs. Coates gave me this manuscript she remarked that although her great-grandsire was a very well educated man, he wrote a very bad hand, and that I might be puzzled now and then in getting at his meaning. I found this to be true, and would not like to say that I succeeded in interpreting all of his modern hieroglyphics. When I placed the manuscript in your hands I felt sure that Lewis and Clark, Pike, and Henry and Thompson, as well as other explorers, had made you so familiar with the country gone over by Major Fowler, that you could with comparative ease master its chirographic difficulties. In this I was right; but I do remember how, with your constantly replenished pipe, you sat in my library, and smoked and puzzled over this manuscript. A distinguished host once assured his guest that the more raw turnips he ate, the more water he would drink, and that the more water he drank, the more turnips he would eat. With a touch of similarity, you smoked and read, and read and smoked, with manifest indications of successful or unsuccessful interpretations of the text, as your puffs were rapid or slow. It might be hard to say whether you smoked most or read most, but you finally mastered the manuscript; and whether you did so by smoking out the uninterpretable hieroglyphics, or got rid of them by other means, does not matter. While a cloud of smoke may not seem to be the best means of clearing up the obscurity of a manuscript, it is the known result here considered, if not the philosophy of its action.

Pioneers by the name of Fowler were early in Kentucky, and some of them were the owners of large bodies of land. In 1783, Alexander Fowler entered 10,000 acres on the Little Kentucky river; and in 1784, John Fowler, who was the first member of Congress from Ashland District, located 1536 acres on Brush creek and on the dividing ridge between Pitman's creek and Robertson's run. I do not know whether Jacob Fowler was of the family of these Fowlers, but he was certainly akin to them in so far as the love and ownership of lands were concerned. Besides other possessions, he owned 2000 acres of the site of the present city of Covington, Kenton Co., Ky. He was one of the pioneers of what afterward became the county of Kenton, before the city of Covington was incorporated. A census of the male inhabitants of this locality shows him to have been residing here in 1810, with his sons Edward and Benjamin. Had he been permitted to retain these Covington lands, he might have become a multi-millionaire. His kind heart, however, led him to become the indorser of those who made a clean sweep of his fine estate. A large double brick dwelling house, handsomely furnished, in the midst of ample grounds, planted with trees and shrubbery, flowers and blue-grass, went with his lands to pay the debts of others. Had he written his name as indorser as illegibly as he wrote the names of others in his Journal, there might have been some ground for what lawyers call the plea of *non est factum*, to clear him of liability. But such was not the case, and his security for others swept away his large estate.

Major Fowler was born in New York, in 1765, and came to Kentucky in early life, a fine specimen of physical manhood, fully equipped for the office and duties of a surveyor. His surveying instruments were the best of their day, and elicited no little envy from those who used the common Jacob's staff and compass, and chain of the times. He had the reputation of being an accomplished surveyor, and did much in this line for the United States government. His surveying extended to the great plains and mountains of the far West, before civilization had reached these distant wilds. He was there when wild animals and wilder savages were the only tenants of the wilderness.

Major Fowler married the widow Esther Sanders, *née* de Vie, of Newport, Ky. She was of French descent, and a lady of great beauty and accomplishments. She made his home one of happiness and hospitality. She sometimes accompanied him on his surveying expeditions and bore domestic charms to the tent in which they lived, as she did to the palatial mansion at home. She was a woman of fine business capacity, who, when her husband was not at home, attended to his affairs, and especially to his farm in the suburbs of Covington. Here fine stock and abundant crops owed much to her constant care and supervision. The grapes that grew on the place were made into wine and the apples into cider, in accordance with the knowledge she had inherited from her French ancestors. Her great-grandchildren of today tell of the life of the camp, when she was with her husband in his surveying expeditions. The tent floor was nicely carpeted; a comfortable bed invited repose after the toil of the day; dainty china, bright cut glass, and shining silverware, handsome enough to be preserved as family heirlooms by their descendants, were used on the camp table. It was something of Parisian life in the dreary wilderness.

Major Fowler died in Covington in the year 1850. His life as a surveyor and explorer in the West subjected him to many hardships, but a constitution naturally vigorous was preserved with care until he reached his eighty-sixth year. He has numerous descendants in Kentucky, Ohio, and other States, some of whom occupy high social positions. Mrs. Coates, to whom I am indebted for this manuscript Journal, is, in the paternal line, the granddaughter of Captain John Cleve Symmes, author of the "Theory of Concentric Spheres," 12mo, Cincinnati, 1826, and great-grandniece of Hon. John Cleve Symmes, a member of Congress from New Jersey, who purchased of the United States government that vast body of land in the State of Ohio, lying on the north bank of the Ohio river between the two Miamis. With the knowledge and consent of her father, the late Americus Symmes, she gave me the manuscript in the belief that I would make some good use of it. After thinking for a time that I would place it among the Filson Club Publications, I changed my mind and turned it over to you to be published. I think this is the best use I could have made of the manuscript, and I shall now wait with impatience until I see your work published in the best style of Francis P. Harper, and read your ample notes and comments, which I doubt not will be after the inimitable manner of your Lewis and Clark, your Pike, and your Henry and Thompson.

Truly,

R. T. Durrett.

The MS. which I received from Colonel Durrett is entitled: "memorandom of the voige by land from fort Smith to the Rockey mountains"—and is the most like those mountains of any I have ever undertaken to overcome. My eminent friend does not exaggerate the difficulty of deciphering the characters which he aptly styles "hieroglyphics," and which have hitherto kept this writing a sealed book. The text begins verso of the title, and ostensibly runs pp. 1–264, but pagination is once skipped and twice duplicated. The folios may be called of square notepaper size, nearly that of a small quarto book—8 × 6½ inches for pp. 1–180, but larger, nearly 9 × 7, for the rest. The ragged edges make exact measurements impracticable, Father Time's paper-mill having turned out a deckel-edged product, so fashionable nowadays. The sheets, of four pages or two folios each, are gathered in 16-page packets, the outsides of which are now much soiled—indeed, the rough, unruled surfaces are all darkened with the dust of three-quarters of a century, and the ink is faded to match the same subdued monotone, except in places where it recedes to the vanishing point. The writing is upon both sides of the paper; and the whole effect, if it could be facsimiled, would be a bibliomaniac's dream of delight.

At first sight, this manuscript appears illegible; no one can read it off-hand. Nevertheless, this writing proves readable upon sufficient study of the alphabetic characters which Fowler invented to suit himself, like that classic old Theban Cadmus, or his modern imitator, Cherokee Sequoiah. I managed to master it under the agreeable circumstances of my visit to Louisville, to which my host on that occasion has so pleasantly alluded in the letter printed above; and after that my secretary also proved herself equal to the task when she took the matter in hand to copy for the press. There are hardly a dozen words in which doubt attaches to a single letter, and probably not half as many have proven altogether illegible.

Fowler wrote a large sprawling hand, as may be judged by the fact that only 174 of these small open pages are required to print his 264 folios, with my 176 notes. He commonly conforms to the requirements of dotted i and crossed t, but otherwise strikes out for himself in the formation of letters. His most original invention is an r which would puzzle Œdipus, as it is always a careful n; most of his short-stroke characters look alike in their resemblance to bends of the Arkansaw river on a map, and his long strokes seem as if they had been struck by lightning. The incessant capitals are flourished elaborately, and not confined to initial letters. Fowler is also fond of capping little words, as if he thought they needed such help to hold up their heads with big ones, and equally apt to begin proper names, sentences, and paragraphs with lowercase letters. This style of composition appears on the printed page, which faithfully imitates every peculiarity of the original which can be set with an ordinary font of type. The syntax is the sort which has been happily called "dash dialect"—Fowler has no other punctuation than the dash, excepting a sporadic period here and there, usually misplaced, and an occasional stab at the paper which is neither one thing nor another, and may therefore be overlooked. His spelling speaks so well for itself in print that little need be said on that score. Its entire originality, its effusive spontaneity, its infinite variety, will charm the reader while it puzzles him, and make the modern manufacturer of Dialect despair of his most ingenious craft. Aside from sheer slips of the pen, by which Fowler often misses letters, as in writing "campe," "caped," "capped," or "capted" for *camped*, there is a particular point to which I may call attention as the most character-istic—in fact, the diagnostic—feature of his composition. It is that habitual omission of final *y* which makes the definite article do duty for the third personal pronoun nominative; and when this is followed by a misspelled verb simulating a noun, some curious locutions result. Thus, "the Road" stands for *they rode;* "the Ware," for *they were;* "the Cold," for *they could;* "the Head," for *they had;* "the Maid," for *they made*—and so on, to the end of the book.

But it is needless to pursue this alluring theme; the reader may turn to the text which follows this feeble preface so strenuously, and see for himself with what a *tour de force* our ingenious author managed to evade what we now call good grammar. I have found more than one reason for transferring this curious copy to type with the utmost verbality, literality, and punctuality of which the com-positor is capable. In the first place, it tickled my fancy so that I wished others to enjoy the same sensation—for is it not said that our joys are doubled by sharing them, as our sorrows are halved by the same process? Again, to prolong these pleasantries, I may say that I thought this would be a good way to show that awesome deference which I ought to feel for certain captious critics of former works with which my name is associated, whose green-eyed strabismus has seen me in the light of entirely too good an editor—that is to say, who have complimented me by their censure for making my authors too intelligible, too attractive, and altogether too readable, by the way I dressed them for the press.

So I determined to submit the pure text of Fowler's Journal to the discernment of competent critics of literary wares, as well as to the lack of that quality in fussy fault-finders, and let everybody see how some manuscript looks when it is printed just as it is written. I do not vaunt this specimen as unique in any respect except the hand-writing, a sample of which is reproduced. [The sample is not reproduced in this edition.] The article is much like others of Fowler's times and circumstances; it is only a little off the average syntax and orthography of that period, with a few more capitals and dashes than were then usual. I know authors of our own day whose copy would turn out a good deal like Fowler's if the printer did not fix it up for them. They are mostly the ones who damn instead of blessing the artists of the art preservative of arts. Few women, for example, can spell quite like the dictionaries; fewer still can punctuate properly; and fewest of all persons of either sex in the world are those authors, even among professional literarians, who would like or could afford to see themselves set up in print exactly as they write themselves down. There is said to be a day coming when the secrets of all hearts shall be revealed, the wicked shall tremble, and they shall say to the mountains, "fall on us"—or words to that effect. I cite the passage from early memory, not having the author in hand, and have not verified the quotation; but I will risk anything of that sort, provided the day never comes when the secrets of the printing office shall be revealed. I am at peace with my God, my neighbor, and myself; but—I am an author.

If we turn from the form to the substance of Fowler's Journal, and ask to see the bill of lading, curious to know what useful or valuable information is contained in so singular a vehicle of conveyance, it may be confidently said that this "prairie schooner" is well freighted for a "voige" on the highway of Americana; for the cargo is a novel and notable contribution to our knowledge of early commercial venture and pioneering adventure in the Great West. It is simply a story of the trader and trapper, unsupported by the soldier, un-impeded by the priest, and in no danger from the politician. The scene is set in the wilderness; the time is when pack-animals are driven across the stage, before the first wheels rolled over the plains from the States to Santa Fé; and the actors have very real parts to perform.

From the respective dates of Pursley, of Lalande, and of Pike, whose several travels were among the first if not the earliest overland from the United States to the Spanish settlements, on the part of American citizens—from the opening years of the century to the

1821–22 of Fowler—various parties were on the Arkansaw in what are now Kansas and Colorado. But the records of where they went or what they did? That is the question. Ezekiel Williams, James Workman, Samuel Spencer, sole and shadowy survivors of Coyner's "Lost Trappers," are only uneasy spirits flitting from the Missouri to Mexico and California in an apocryphal book, never materializing out of fable-land into historical environment. Wherever other American trappers or traders may have gone on the Arkansaw or even the Rio Grande in those days, and whatever they may have done, Fowler was first to forge another sound link in the chain which already reached from Pike to Long. The latter's justly celebrated expedition came down the Arkansaw and the Canadian in 1820. Pike ascended the main river from its great bend to its sources in 1806, the same year that his lieutenant, Wilkinson, descended this stream from the point where he parted from his captain. For the lower reaches of the river we have Thomas Nuttall's Journal of Travels into the Arkansa Territory, during the year 1819, and various other accounts. But I know of no record, earlier in date than Fowler's, of continuous ascent of the river from Fort Smith to the present position of Pueblo in Colorado. He meandered the whole course of the Arkansaw between the points named, except his cut-off of a small portion by the Verdigris trail. One of his men, Lewis Dawson, who was killed by a grizzly bear at the mouth of the Purgatory—and who, let us hope, left that place for happier hunting-grounds—may not have been the first white American buried in Colorado soil; but the record of a prior funeral would be far to seek. Whose was the first habitable and inhabited house on the spot where Pueblo now stands? Fowler's, probably; for Pike's stockade was hardly a house, and Jim Beckwourth came twenty years after Fowler. The Taos Trail from Santa Fé through the Sangre de Cristo Pass to the Arkansaw at Pueblo was well known to the Spaniards when Fowler's party traversed it in the opposite direction; but we have no American itinerary of that passage at an earlier date than his. When Fowler ascended the Rio Grande to Hot Spring creek in the San Juan range, he followed a Spanish road; but never before had an American expedition been so near the sources of that great river Del Norte, and not till many years afterward did any such prolong Fowler's traces upward. The greater part of Fowler's homeward journey from Taos to Fort Osage will doubtless prove as novel to his readers as it was unexpected by his editor. South of the Arkansaw, his trail was neither by the way he had gone before, nor by either of those roads which were soon to be established and become well known; for he came neither by the Cimarron nor the Raton route, but took a straighter course than either, between the two, over Chico Rico Mesa and thence along Two Butte creek to the Arkansaw on the Kansan-Coloradan border. Again, when Fowler left the Arkansaw to strike across Kansas, he did not take up the direct route which caravans were about to blaze as the Santa Fé Trail from Missouri through Council Grove to Great Bend; but went a roundabout way, looping far south to heads of the Whitewater and Verdigris rivers before he crossed the Neosho to make for the Missouri below the mouth of the Kansas.

This bare outline of the way Fowler went in twice crossing the Plains, to and from the Rocky mountains, suffices to show that, taken as a whole, it was not only the first but also the last such itinerary of which we have any knowledge; for if this route has since been retraversed in its entirety, time has obliterated all sign of such an adventure.

Another point is to be scored in connection with Fowler's unique performance. The date is a critical one in the history of the whole subject. That elusive "Red river" which Pike sought in vain in 1806 was only the year before Fowler found by Long to be the Canadian fork of the Arkansaw, instead of that separate tributary of the Mississippi which Long imagined he was descending till he reached its confluence with the same stream which the other detachment of his party followed down. Just at the time when Long had finished his exploration, and Fowler was leading his people home from their wide wandering, the Santa Fé trade was taking definite shape. Like every other such enterprise, this one went through its tentative stages of hesitancy and disconcert, before its final organization as a regular industry; and if any year can be named as that of complete equipment for the business, it is that of 1822. Fowler was thus a factor in the beginnings of a commerce which grew by what it fed upon to the immense proportions it had acquired when it was checked by the troubles of 1846.

Whatever be deemed the merit or demerit of Fowler's work as a whole, viewed in the light of a contribution to the history of Western adventure in connection with the fur trade, I can attest the coherency and consequence of the narrative now before us. The author tells a plain, straightforward story, and never fails to make it intelligible. He never loses the thread of his discourse, never tangles it into an irrelevant skein, and holds himself well in hand through all the asperities he experienced. He is a reasonable sort of a writer, if not a very ready one. I have had little trouble in trailing him from start to finish, for all that compass-points uncorrected for magnetic variation, and distances chained only in the sensations of a tired traveler, are not among the "constants of nature"—especially in the mountains; and I am satisfied that his route is laid down correctly in my notes. The sign is a little dim here and there, in some of the cross-country laps, but we never lose it. Fowler had the good eye for topography to be expected of a professional surveyor, and I only wish that some other persons whose peregrinations I have had occasion to follow had exercised powers of observation equal to those which Fowler displayed under arduous exigencies of trade and travel.

Thus far by way of introducing to the public the hitherto unknown author of a new contribution to Americana, which I hope may find that favor which I believe it deserves.

The task of copying Fowler's Journal *v. l. p.* was intrusted to an expert, Mrs. Mary B. Anderson, to whom acknowledgments are due for the result. The copy was made in my absence from home last summer, during which the lady was left entirely to her own resources in making out the manuscript; and subsequent critical comparison of the transcription with the original served mainly to show its beauty as well as accuracy. The Index is also her careful handiwork. [Replaced by a new index in this edition.]

E. C.

1726 N STREET, WASHINGTON, D.C.,
   January 1, 1898.

Memorandom of The Voige by Land from Fort Smith to The Rockey Mountains.

thorsday 6th Sept 1821

We Set out[1] from fort Smith[2] on the arkensaw[3] and Crossing that River pased threw a bottom of Rich Land Well timbered and much

[1] [When he reached the end of his *Memorandum*, Fowler placed the beginning of the "Voige" in Covington, Kentucky, and dated it from June 14, 1821, rather than from September 6. W. Julian Fessler suggested that the opening portion of the *Journal* was written "after a considerable lapse of time." W. Julian Fessler, ed., "Jacob Fowler's Journal: Oklahoma Section," *Chronicles of Oklahoma*, VIII (June 1930), 183 n.]

[2] Present name of the town which has grown up on the site of the original military post, in Sebastian Co., Ark., about 5 m. S. W. of Van Buren, on the right bank of the Arkansaw river, at the mouth of Poteau river, immediately on the W. border of the State, where the river passes from the Indian Territory into Arkansas; lat. 35° 22′ N., long. 94° 28′ W.; pop. in 1890, 11,311. The original name of the then important frontier locality was Belle Pointe. "The site of Fort Smith was selected by Major Long, in the fall of 1817, and called Belle Point in allusion to its peculiar beauty. It occupies an elevated point of land, immediately below the junction of the Arkansa and the Poteau, a small tributary from the southwest. Agreeably to the orders of General Smith, then commanding the 9th military department, a plan of the proposed work was submitted to Major Bradford, at that time, and since commandant at the post, under whose superintendence the works have been in part completed" in Sept., 1820: Long's Exp. ii, 1823, p. 260, where description of the place follows.

From this starting-point our author proceeds on the direct road to the Neosho river, vicinity of present Fort Gibson, Ind. Terr.

[The decision to establish a fort in this area was made by General Thomas A. Smith, commander of the Ninth Military Department, and William Clark, governor of Missouri Territory, in the summer of 1817. The site was selected by Major William Bradford and Major Stephen H. Long, and Camp Smith was established at the end of November. In August and September 1821, Bradford was still in command at Fort Smith. A new fort was built on a reservation of three hundred acres in 1838. The buildings, which fronted the river, formed a hollow square terminated by strong blockhouses at opposite corners. At one time the fort was the chief supply depot for the western army posts. During the Civil War, in April 1863, it was seized by Arkansas troops. The fort was abandoned in 1871, and the land on which it stood was donated to the town of Fort Smith. Clarence E. Carter, ed., *Territorial Papers of the United States* (26 vols.; Washington, 1934–62), XIX, 3, 8; *Niles' Weekly Register*, XIII (November 8, 1817), 176; Grant Foreman, *Indians and Pioneers: The Story of the American Southwest Before 1830* (Norman: University of Oklahoma Press, 1936), pp. 48–51; Edwin C. Bearss, "In Quest of Peace on the Indian Border: The Establishment of Fort Smith," *Arkansas Historical Quarterly*, XXIII (Summer 1964), 123–53; Carolyn Thomas Foreman, "William Bradford," *Arkansas Historical Quarterly*, XIII (Winter 1954), 341–51; LeRoy R. Hafen, "The Bean-Sinclair Party of Rocky Mountain Trappers, 1830–32," *Colorado Magazine*, XXXI (July 1954), 161–71; Edwin James, comp., "An account of an expedition from Pittsburgh to the Rocky Mountains, performed in the years 1819, 1820," in *Early Western Travels*, ed. Reuben G. Thwaites (32 vols.; Cleveland: Arthur H. Clark, 1904–1907), XVI, 187–88; and Richard G. Wood, "Stephen Harriman Long at Belle Pointe," *Arkansas Historical Quarterly*, XIII (Winter 1954), 338–40.]

3 [The European discoverer of the Arkansas River approached from the southwest. Coronado reached the stream about the end of June, 1541. Almost immediately afterward De Soto reached a lower portion of the river from the northeast. During the centuries that followed those initial discoveries, the river was given a great variety of names. The name by which it is known today is apparently of Indian origin. Marquette, who, like De Soto, approached it from the northeast, wrote of a "grand Village nommée AKamsca" and his map shows a place labeled "Dakansea." "Decouverte de quelques pays et nations de l'Amerique septentrionale," in Melchisedech Thévenot, *Recueil de voyages de Mr Thevenot* (Paris, 1681), pp. 37, 42, and map facing p. 1. Tonti, reporting the explorations of La Salle, mentioned "les *AKancéas*" several times (Henri de Tonti, *Dernieres Descouvertes dans l'Amerique septentrionale de M. de la Sale* [Paris, 1687], pp. 161–63, 165, 300, 314, 331). Charlevoix, who explored the Louisiana country in 1721–22, mentioned the "Akansas" and "Pays des Akansas," and on his map, which was drawn by Bellin, located both "Akansas" and "Rv. des Akansas" (Pierre F. X. Charlevoix, *Histoire et description generale de la Nouvelle France* [6 vols.; Paris, 1744], I, 446, 464, and map facing p. 1). The Bellin map was the basis for Map No. 100, "A New and Accurate Map of Louisiana," in Emanuel Bowen, *A Complete System of Geography* (2 vols.; London, 1747), II, between pp. 620 and 621, in which "les Acansa" were mentioned. An apparently erroneous spelling, the "Riv. des Acausas," was introduced, however. The name was assigned to the river and received its modern form, "Arkansas" and "Riviere des Arkansas," in the work of Le Page du Pratz, who lived in and explored the

Kaine [4]—thence over Low Ridges the land poor and in some places Rockey—at 30 miles crosed the tallecaw [5] a Crick about 150 feet Wid Large bottoms on bothe Sides and at ten miles farther Crosed the Illinios River [6] about 80 yds Wide and about one mile farther Stoped for the night at Beens [7] Salt Workes—this is the Second night

country between 1718 and 1734. Antoine Simon Le Page du Pratz, *Histoire de la Louisiane* (3 vols.; Paris, 1758), I, 6, 7, 149–52; II, 243; and map, I, between pp. 138 and 139. (The courtesy of the New York Public Library, Rare Books Division, in providing all sources cited in this note is gratefully acknowledged.)]

[4] The common cane, *Arundinaria macrosperma*, which forms extensive brakes.

[Canebrakes found on the lower Neosho River in 1828 were small in comparison with those farther south. The ordinary plant was from seven to ten feet tall. Along the Neosho, Arkansas, and Illinois rivers the brakes were so dense as to make travel through them difficult and sometimes impossible. John F. McDermott, ed., "Isaac McCoy's Second Exploring Trip in 1828," *Kansas Historical Quarterly*, XIII (August 1945), 439–40.]

[5] Tahlequah or Talequah, one of several small tributaries of the Arkansaw from the N., below the Illinios river; on which latter is the town of Tahlequah, capital of the Cherokee Nation, Indian Terr., about 45 m. N. W. of Fort Smith.

[Tahlequah is the seat of Cherokee County, Oklahoma. The stream was Sallisaw Creek. "It is nearer twenty miles distant from the Illinois than ten, which is the distance given by Fowler. Vian Creek is about ten miles below the Illinois, but could not have possibly been the stream mentioned, since it is very narrow whereas the Sallisaw is much larger and fits the width measurement given in the journal. So apparently, Major Fowler wrote this entry after a considerable lapse of time during which period he forgot the order of crossing the two, or Bayou Viande was so small at that time of the year as to escape his notice completely." Fessler, "Jacob Fowler's Journal," p. 183 n.]

[6] Illinois river, the largest tributary of the Arkansaw from the N. between Fort Smith and Fort Gibson: see Pike, ed. of 1895, p. 558, and add: "The Illinois is called by the Osages, Eng-wah-con-dah or Medicine-stone creek," Long, ii, 1823, p. 255. Fowler crosses the Illinois some 6 or 8 m. from its confluence with the Arkansaw.

[It is not known by whom this stream was named. It seems reasonable to assume, however, that it was given its name by French traders and trappers from the Illinois country. Fessler, "Jacob Fowler's Journal," p. 183 n.]

[7] Bean's or Bean and Saunders' salt works were begun in the spring of 1820 about a mile up a small creek which flows into the Illinois at or near the place where Fowler crosses the latter, some 6 m. from the Arkansaw; description in Long, ii, 1823, p. 254.

[In 1817, Mark and Richard H. Bean settled about two and one-half miles above the mouth of Salt Creek, a small tributary of the Illinois River, seven miles north of Gore, Sequoyah County, Oklahoma. They improved their farm with a double log cabin, Negro quarters, stables, two drying houses, a large salt house for deposits, and sheds over two rows or kettles at two salt springs. In

Since We left the fort—the the Workes one Small Well With a few
kittles about 55 gallons of Watter make a bushil of Salt and the Well
afords Watter to boil the kittles about three days in the Weake   Been
and Sanders Has permission of the govem [government] to Worke
the Salt Spring—the Sell the Salt at one dollar per Bushil—from
Heare We pased over Some High poor Hills Some valleys and Some
pirarie lands about twenty miles to a large bottom Well Covered in
parts With Caine and Well timbered—threw Which We pased
about Eight miles to grand River or Six bull.[8]   this is fine bold
Streem of Clear Watter about 150 yd Wide Which We forded but
not Without Some doupts—the Watter Runing With great force—
about one mile above the mouth of this River is the mouth of the
virdegree[9] a River of about one Hundred yds Wide deep and muddy

---

1819, Major William Bradford induced them to make salt for the garrison at
Fort Smith, and it was doubtless at this time that Reuben Saunders became
associated with them. Before 1826, Saunders sold his interest in the business to the
Beans, who continued to operate it until 1828, when the territory in which it was
located was ceded to the Cherokee Indians and white people were removed from
it. The Bean brothers presented a claim against the government which was not
paid until 1857. Carolyn Thomas Foreman, "The Bean Family," *Chronicles of
Oklahoma*, XXXII (Autumn 1954), 308–25; Edward F. Murray, "Mountain
Men—George Nidever," *Colorado Magazine*, X (May 1933), 94–95; Harlin M.
Fuller and LeRoy R. Hafen, eds., *The Journal of Captain John R. Bell* (Glendale,
Calif.: Arthur H. Clark, 1957), 272; James, "An account of an expeditlon,"
XVI, 286; and Carter, *Territorial Papers*, XV, 50; XIX, 341, 559–60, 617.]

[8] The Neosho, for which see Pike, ed. of 1895, pp. 395, 397–401, etc. "The
Neosho, or *Grand* river, better known to the hunters by the singular designation of
the *Six Bulls*," Long, ii, 1823, p. 253. This is a name which I missed in editing
Pike. On the left bank of the Neosho, near its mouth, is Fort Gibson, which was
not in existence in 1821.

[The name *Neosho* comes from two Osage words, *ne*, meaning "water," and
osho, meaning "bowl." Applied to the stream, it means "deep places" or "holes
shaped like bowls." To the early French traders the river was known as Le
Grande, and to Americans it was Grand River. The Osage Indians called it
Ni-U-Sho, to which is given the meaning "Waters (colored) like cow hide." Why
it was called Six Bulls is not known. The stream rises in Morris County, Kansas,
runs southeast, and empties into the Arkansas River in northeast Muskogee
County, Oklahoma. Fessler, "Jacob Fowler's Journal," p. 184 n.; Alice S. Smith,
"Through the Eyes of My Father," *Kansas Historical Collections*, XVII (1926–
28), 708 n.; and John Joseph Mathews, *The Osages: Children of the Middle
Waters* (Norman: University of Oklahoma Press, 1961), pp. 181, 552, 812.]

[9] The Verdigris, Vermilion, Wasetihoge, or Wassaju river, for which see Pike,
ed. of 1895, p. 400 and p. 555. Its confluence with the Arkansaw is about the

at the mouth and up it to the Rapids[10] about four miles Wheare there is a trading House.   but we Stoped at the trading Hous of Conl Hugh glann[11] about mile up the virdegree Wheare We Remained till the 25th Sept makeing a Raingment for our gurney to the mountains—Heare five of our Hunters Left us and Went Home this Sircumstance much dispereted more of our men—tho We Still determined to purced—and on the 25th of Sept 1821 We found our Selves 20 men in all.[12] and under the Command of Conl Hugh glann

---

distance said in the text above that of the Neosho. For a few miles from its mouth it forms a part of the boundary between the Cherokee and Creek Nations, and is then crossed by the Mo., Kas. and Tex. R. R., Gibson Station being about 7 m. N. W. of Fort Gibson. Fowler will proceed approximately up the Verdigris for a long distance before turning more westward to reach the Arkansaw again.

[The Verdigris River rises in Chase County, Kansas, flows south, and empties into the Arkansas about a mile above the point at which the Neosho enters that stream. The name is probably a combination of two French words, *vert*, meaning "green," and *gris*, meaning "gray," from the green-gray color of the rocks in its bed. The Osage Indians called the stream Wa-Ce To'n-Xo-E, gray-green-bark-waters. Fessler, "Jacob Fowler's Journal," p. 184 n.; and Mathews, *The Osages* p. 181.]

10 [Joseph Bougie (or Bogy) established a trading post in 1819 at the rapids on the Verdigris about four miles above its mouth (Louise Barry, comp., "Kansas before 1854: A Revised Annals," *Kansas Historical Quarterly*, XXVII [Winter 1961], 498). Other sources maintain that Charles Bougie established this trading post. Much information on the subject is recorded by Nuttall. Fessler, "Jacob Fowler's Journal," p. 184 n.; Thomas Nuttall, "A Journal of Travels into the Arkansa Territory, during the year 1819," in Thwaites, *Early Western Travels*, XIII, 234–37, 241, 244–46, 255–56, 260, 263, 276–77; and Foreman, *Indians and Pioneers*, pp. 16, 31 n.]

11 Hugh Glenn or Glen, whom Fowler calls "Glann," is readily identified as a well-known Indian trader of those days. "A party of men accompanying Mr. Hugh Glen on his way from Fort Smith, to the trading house at the mouth of the Verdigris," Long's Exp. ii, 1823, p. 171, with other remarks on p. 172. "5th [Sept., 1820]. At ten o'clock we arrived at Mr. Glen's trading house near the Verdigris, about a mile above its confluence with the Arkansa. We were hospitably received by the interpreter, a Frenchman, who informed us that Mr. Glen was absent on a visit to Belle Point," *ibid.*, p. 251. As we next discover, "Conl. Glann" commanded our present expedition.

[See also Fuller and Hafen, *Journal of Captain John R. Bell*, pp. 269–70, 272, 275, 279, 280.]

12 From the above defective list of 20 persons, taken in connection with information regarding their names to be found further on in the book, we arrive at the following approximately correct roster of the party:

1. Colonel HUGH GLENN, in command.

With mager Jacob Fowler Robert Fowler   Battis Roy   Battis Peno
george Duglas   Nat Pryer[13]   Bono   Barbo   Lewis Dauson
Taylor   Richard   Walters   Ward   Jesey   vanbeber   Slover

---

2. Major JACOB FOWLER, the journalist, second in command.

3. ROBERT FOWLER, brother of Jacob Fowler.

4. BAPTISTE ROY, interpreter.

5. BAPTISTE PENO. (French name, no doubt mispelled.)

6. GEORGE DOUGLAS.

7. NATHANIEL PRYOR, ex-Sergeant of Lewis and Clark's Expedition.

8. —— BONO. (French name, no doubt misspelled, possibly Bonhomme.)

9. —— BARBO. (French name, no doubt misspelled, possibly Barbu.)

10. LEWIS DAWSON. (Fatally injured by a bear, Nov. 13, 1821; died Nov. 16.)

11. —— TAYLOR.

12. RICHARD WALTERS.

13. ELI WARD.

14. JESSE VAN BIBER.

15. —— SLOVER.

16. —— SIMPSON.

17. DUDLEY MAXWELL.

18. —— FINDLEY.

19. BAPTISTE MORAN.

20. PAUL, a negro belonging to Jacob Fowler.

[Although the roster was correct at this time, the number increased to twenty-one, probably on September 29, and for a few days (October 8–14) it was twenty-two, with the inclusion of an Indian. Two entries on January 1 and 2, 1822, the former, dictated by Glenn, the latter Fowler's own, show that Glenn and four other men left together for Santa Fe. At that time six men were trapping in the mountains, one had died, and nine remained in camp. The latter sixteen are identified by name. The five who departed to cross the mountains included one who is not named in the roster.]

13 The most interesting of the above names is that of Nathaniel Pryor, of whose identity with the sergeant of Lewis and Clark I have no doubt: see L. and C., ed. of 1893, p. 254, delete the query there, and add: Nathaniel Pryor of Kentucky became an Ensign of the U. S. Army Feb. 27, 1807; Second Lieutenant May 3, 1808; resigned April 1, 1810; was appointed First Lieutenant of the 44th Inf. Aug. 30, 1813; promoted to be Captain Oct. 1, 1814; and honorably discharged June 15, 1815. See also my article, "Letters of William Clark and Nathaniel Pryor," in Annals of Iowa, 3d ser., Vol. I, No. 8, Jan., 1895, pp. 613–620, for an account of Ensign Pryor's disastrous attempt to convey the Mandan chief Shahaka from St. Louis, Mo., to the Mandan villages on the Missouri. [This paragraph was part of note 12 in Coues's original edition.]

[Much more information about the members of the party is known today than was known by Coues. See Andrew F. Rolle, "Isaac Slover," in LeRoy R. Hafen, ed., *Mountain Men and the Fur Trade of the Far West* (6 vols.; Glendale, Calif.:

Arthur H. Clark, 1965–68), I, 367–71; Harry R. Stevens, "Hugh Glenn," *ibid.*, II, 161–74; Raymond W. Settle, "Nathaniel Pryor," *ibid.*, II, 277–84; Settle, "Nathaniel Miguel Pryor," *ibid.*, II, 285–88; Settle, "Jacob Fowler," *ibid.*, III, 119–30; and Bernice Martin, "The Mystery of Paul," *Frontier Times*, XLII (June–July 1968), 23, 42–43.

Bono and Barbo were surely Jacques Bono and Joseph Barbo, two men named on Glenn's license of August 5, 1821. Paul, according to an ingenious interpretation by Bernice Martin (based on a fresh reading of the journal), developed a spirit of personal freedom on the expedition and ultimately remained in the West as a free man.

Coues was in error in identifying Fowler's "Nat Pryer" as Captain Nathaniel Pryor, "ex-Sergeant of Lewis and Clark's Expedition." He was Nathaniel Miguel Pryor, probably the captain's nephew. Born near the Falls of the Ohio (Louisville) in Kentucky between 1798 and 1805, he moved to Missouri about 1820. In the fall of 1821 he was living on the lower Verdigris near the trading posts, where he joined the Glenn-Fowler expedition. Pryor is mentioned four times in the journal, on September 25 and December 3, 1821, and June 14 and 16, 1822. Nothing is known of his activities for the next three years. In the summer of 1825 he was again in the neighborhood of the Verdigris trading posts, where he and three companions outfitted themselves to go to New Mexico on a trapping expedition. On August 7 at Walnut Creek, near the top of the big bend of the Arkansas River, he met George C. Sibley's Santa Fe Trail survey party. A week later Pryor left them and went on to Santa Fe, taking two of Sibley's men with him. In 1827 he joined James Ohio Pattie and trapped along the Gila River. Late in the year he and his companions, having lost their horses to the Indians, set out on foot for California. After intense suffering they reached Santa Catalina mission on March 12. They were arrested and thrown into prison, where they remained about one year. On being released, Pryor settled in Los Angeles, where he died in 1850. Kate L. Gregg, *The Road to Santa Fe* (Albuquerque: University of New Mexico Press, 1952), pp. 22, 37, 70, 81–82, 255; Hubert Howe Bancroft, *History of California* (6 vols.; San Francisco: A. L. Bancroft, 1884–88), II, 554; III, 168; IV, 785; and Carter, *Territorial Papers*, XIV, XIX, XX, *passim*.

Glenn's license reads as follows:

WILLIAM BRADFORD

Major in the United States' Army, Commander of the Military Forces of the United States on the Arkansas River

To All whom it may concern—Be it Known that Whereas Hugh Glenn has made application for a License to trade with Indians in Amity with the United States at the following Positions viz. At the Falls of the Verdigris—at the Mouth of the Red Fork—at the Thousand Islands north side—at Pikes' third Fork north side—and at the head of the Arkansas north side at or near the Mountains—Traders Hugh Glenn, Jacob Fowler, Baptiste Roy, Robert Fowler —Handy—Jacques Bono. Louis Rivar—Joseph Barbo—Absalom Holloway— Jonathan Padget—Francis Arguet—Henry Duval—Baptiste Pino—Julian Pera—Francois Quenville—Newill (Blk Man) Paul (Blk Man) Richard Walters—And has given bond according to law for the due observance of all such regulations as now are or hereafter may be established for the government

Simpson   Maxwill   Findley Battis moran and Pall a black
man the property of mager Fowler we Head thirty Horses and mules
Seventen of Which traps and goods for the Indean traid—and Each
man mounted on Horsback—We Left the traiding House in the
afternoon—North 50 West about five miles to a Small Crick Which
Runs West in to the virdegree—the Bottom between the Six bull and
verdegree is High and Rich Well timbered With Some Caine and is
about one and a Half miles Wide to the Hills—from What We Cold
Learn there is no Caine above this on the arkensaw—We pased to
day Some Pirarie Cirted With Wood land Some timber on the Crick
it Rained Hard We Packed up our goods and Covered them With
Skins to keep them dry and Piched our tents for the night—Conl
Hugh glann Haveing Left us and gon by the mishenerys,[14] and to
meet us Some Wheare a Head—

26th We Set out Early along the Road Leading to the osage
vilege[15] threw fine Pirarie Lands a little Rolling and Scirted With
timber the ground is Black and Rich and the vew the most delight-

---

of trade and intercourse with the Indian Tribes. License for Two Years is
hereby granted to the said Hugh Glenn to trade with the said Indians according
to the regulations aforesaid   In Testimony whereof I have caused my private
seal to be hereunto affixed   Given under my hand at Fort Smith Arkansas
River the 5th day of August in the year of our Lord One Thousand Eight
Hundred Twenty-one and of the Independence of the United States the
Fortysixth.

W. Bradford, Major
United States Army Comdg.
Arkansas.]

[14] Indian missionaries, several of whose establishments have been located in
this vicinity.

[Glenn visited the Union Mission. It was located on the west bank of the Neosho
River, twenty-five miles above its junction with the Arkansas. Reconnaissance
for the mission had been made in the summer and fall of 1819 by the Reverend
Epaphras Chapman from Connecticut, and the first missionaries reached the site
on November 15, 1820. Glenn was a well-known visitor.]

[15] Approximately up the Verdigris, as already indicated. The road taken is
marked on several maps I have examined. For the Osage village in mention, see
Pike, ed. of 1893, p. 557. This "Arkansaw band" of Osages consisted of those
called "Osages of the Oaks," in Long, ii, p. 251. Their most influential man then,
as in Pike's time, was Clermont, surnamed the "Builder of Towns," and I
suppose that the village now called Claremore, among the Blue Mounds on the
Verdigris, in the Cherokee country, was named for him. In 1820 some of Long's
party were assured "that Clermont had then four wives, and thirty-seven
children! a number . . . which may probably be attributed to this chief by mis-

full We this day maid 20 miles threw the Rain Which Continued all day at night Camped on a Crick about 50 feet Wid Runs West With an Extensive Beed of Stone Coal in its bottom there is Some Wood along the Crick but the Cuntry is mostly Pirarie a little Rolling Scirted With groves of timber Heare the Rain Continued all night [16]—Heare one of our Hunters—Slover Lay out all night but Came in in the morning

27th We Set out Early along the path threw the Pirarie—timber still to be seen in groves and along the Branches—We maid 20 miles and Camped on a Small Crick [17] Well timbered—Heare we found Findley He Left us 2 days ago—and was Heare waiting for us this day was Clear and pleesent Robert Fowler killed a Large Buck—one Hors gave out was left

28th Sept 1821 Rained all day we Remained in Camp—

29th the Weather Clear We Set out Early and was Soon over taken By Conl glann and soon after in Sight of the osage vilege. Heare We Ware delited With a vew of a number of Hills or mounds [18] nearely

---

take," as the narrative sagely adds. Clermont's band are also called "Chaneers," *ibid.*, p. 244, on the authority of Dr. Sibley.

[This was Cashashegra's village, five or six miles northwest of the site of Claremore, Rogers County, Oklahoma, and half a mile southwest of Claremore Hill. A battle between the Osages and the Western Cherokees took place here in 1818; the town and crops were destroyed and some fifty elderly persons and children were carried off. The warfare continued intermittently until 1822. Fessler, "Jacob Fowler's Journal," p. 186 n.; Mathews, *The Osages*, pp. 461–77; Walter B. Douglas, "Manuel Lisa," *Missouri Historical Collections*, III, Nos. 3 and 4 (1911), 233–68, 367–406; and Carter, *Territorial Papers*, XIX, 288–459.]

16 [About thirty years after Coues, Fessler restudied the journal and proposed a different itinerary for the expedition from September 26 to October 4: "The camp of the 26th was on Bull Creek, close to its intersection of the Rogers-Wagoner County line, or three miles west of Neodosha. The distance of this day's march is nearer fifteen miles than twenty as reported." Fessler, "Jacob Fowler's Journal," p. 186 n.]

17 ["At evening of the 27th, the party encamped at the confluence of Dog and Panther Creeks, west of Tiawah, Rogers County. Again the distance traveled is barely fifteen instead of the reported twenty miles." Fessler, "Jacob Fowler's Journal," p. 186 n.]

18 These are the Blue Mounds mentioned in note 15. The several "cricks," which Fowler has spoken of crossing, are inconsiderable tributaries of the Verdigris flowing southerly, as those called Big, Otter, Dog, etc.

of the Same Hight.   from 70 to 80 feet but of diferent Shapes Some Round and pointed like a Stack others squair and flat.   and the top of one neare the vilege Contains about 15 acres of Rich Black land —and great part of the Bluff faced With a parpendickler Rock—so that with but little labour a few men might keep off a large armey— Heare is one of the most delight full peace of Cuntry I Have Ever Seen—of Rich lime stone land mixed With Wood lands the Pirarie is more Exstensive than Woods—

Heare We find not one sole in or about the vilege [19] the Indeans are all gon a buffelow Hunting and are not Exspected to return till in the Winter. We find our Jurney to this place one Continued Corse North 50 W   Heare we Crosed the virdegree [20] and got on Higher grounds and Nearly Covered With Rocks in Some places and Steered North 70 West 10 miles to a small Crick [21] Runing South and Well timbered—Heare We Camped for the night—We Seen this day Some Wild Horses.   game is scars We this day find our Horses two Heavey loaded and Concluded to leave part [of their loads]

30th Sept 1821

We this morning Berryed or Cashed [cached] as the french Call it

[19] [The Indians had gone off on their annual fall buffalo hunt, in which the whole tribe—men, women, and children—participated. They traveled west and northwest to buffalo country in the neighborhood of the Big Bend of the Arkansas River. Customarily they dried a huge amount of meat for the coming winter; secured hides for making lodges, clothing, and moccasins; and returned to their villages before cold weather set in.

When the Little Osage Indians were induced by Pierre Chouteau to settle on the lower Verdigris, they established three towns. A trail from the new towns to their old home on the Osage River in Vernon County, Missouri, was marked and used by Indians and traders alike. This was undoubtedly the trail to which Fowler refers. T. F. Morrison, "Mission Neosho, the First Kansas Mission," *Kansas Historical Quarterly*, IV (August 1935), 227–34; and Mathews, *The Osages*, pp. 365, 391.]

[20] The Verdigris has been crossed from E. to W. a very few miles above the confluence therewith of the Little Verdigris or Caney river, which is now on Fowler's left as he follows it up approximately, but at some distance therefrom, on a general course about N. W. Of the series of its small tributaries, running to his left, the one on which he camps is perhaps Five Mile creek, or the next beyond that.

[21] ["The camp of the 29th and 30th was on Rabb's Creek near its confluence with the Caney River." Fessler, "Jacob Fowler's Journal," p. 187 n.]

32 Bever traps 2 Cases of tobaco and fifty pounds of Brass Wier [22] on the West Bant of the Creek 200 yds above the large Road [23] and 50 below the small path on Which is a Connu [canoe] marked on an oack

october 1th 1821

We Set out Early and Stered North 50 West to the little virdegree Wheare a large Indean Road Crosse it this River is about 30 yds Wide With Clear Watter and High Banks—and large inCampment on the East Side. Heare we Crossed to the West Side and followed the North forke of the Road about one mile to another Branch of the Same River [24] but Not more than ten Steps Wide both Streems Running South With Rich timbered bottom between the boath— after pasing this forke We Stered the Same Corse threw Roling Pirarie ten miles to a mound. to the North and East the Cuntry is a little Rolling mostly Pirarie With timber along the Branches on our left the mountains or High Hills appeer at from four to five miles distance Heare to avoid the Hills Which Continu on our left We Steered N 30 West six mill [miles] and Camped on the little virdegree [25]—Peno Went off to Hunt in the fore part of this day and did not Return—

2nd october 1821 We set out Early and pased over High Leavel Pirarie lands North 45 West three miles to the High Hills Crossing a small Bransh Runing North at the futt of them—We after Some time gained the top of the Hills and found the Cuntry Rolling and partly timbered and partly Pirarie at twelve miles farthe We Crossed the little virdegree again and Camped on the

[22] [These goods confirm the words in Glenn's license that the expedition set out to trade with the Indians on the upper Arkansas River and to trap beaver in the mountains. The items were not appropriate for the Santa Fe trade.]

[23] ["The Little Verdigris is now known as the Caney River. The large Indian road mentioned had doubtless been made by the Osages going to and from the buffalo grounds to the westward." Fessler, "Jacob Fowler's Journal," p. 187 n.]

[24] The smaller one of the main two forks of the Verdigris, running on a general S. E. course from Kansas through the N. E. corner of Oklahoma into the Cherokee country, and joining the Verdigris in the vicinity of the Blue Mounds. Fowler continues up the Little Verdigris.

[25] ["This camp of October 1st was on Caney River, a short distance south of the present city of Bartlesville, county seat of Washington County." Fessler, "Jacob Fowler's Journal," p. 187 n.]

North Bank [26] Heare Duglass got lost in the Evenings Hunt and lay out all night

3rd october 1821   this morning our Horses Ware much Scattered and took us till a late our to Collect them—Duglass found the Way to Camp—and Peno Came in With Some veneson Haveing Killed three deer—Heare we found a large Indean Road going up the Crick and Crossing some of its Branches South 30 West and the Hills being High We followed the Road. the lands poor With Short oack and Hickory for about fifteen miles Wheare the Cuntry begins to appear With fine Rich Piraries Well bordered With Wood lands of a good quality We this day got one deer and Some turkeys   game is getting more plenty—We maid 20 miles and Camped on a Small Crick Running South—[27]

4th october 1821

We Set out Early and at three miles Crossed a Crick 50 feet Wide Running No 45 West—and at about three miles farther in an open Pirarie We found a large Buffelow Bull lying dead Soposed to be killed by the Indeans   We now begin to Hope Soon to kill Some Buffelow our Selves as we Have nothing With us but Salt only What

26 ["The camp for the night of October 2nd was still on the Caney north of the previous night's stand. It was located opposite the mouth of Hickory Creek, in present Osage County." Fessler, "Jacob Fowler's Journal," p. 188 n.]

27 Some obscure tributary of the Little Verdigris, up which river Fowler has come to a point probably not determinable from his itinerary. On crossing the meridian of 96° W. he passed from the Indian Territory into Oklahoma, and is now in the N. W. corner of the latter, in the Osage Reservation, not far from the S. border of Kansas. Hence he will take a general westerly course, through the Osage country, nearly parallel with the Kansas border and Cherokee strip, to the Arkansaw river. I find myself unable to trace this traverse satisfactorily, as neither the courses nor the distances given can be relied upon. I am inclined to think Fowler sometimes reverses the courses of streams—i. e., gives them as they bear from himself, not as they flow. At any rate I cannot identify the several streams he mentions Oct. 3–5. I suppose that, after finishing with the watershed of the Little Verdigris, he crosses some heads of Buck (formerly Suicide) creek, and then Beaver and Little Beaver creeks, whose united streams enter the Arkansaw at the Kaw Agency.

["Camp of October 3rd was at the headwaters of Sand Creek in present Osage County. On the 4th, the party crossed the present Oklahoma-Kansas state line about four miles east of the present site of the Oklahoma town of Frankfort. Camp for that night was made on Beaver Creek, east of Otto, Cowley County, Kansas" (Fessler, "Jacob Fowler's Journal," p. 188 n.). The site of the Kaw Agency is Washunga, Kay County, Oklahoma.]

We kill our Selves. Heare We find our Selves in an oppen and
Exstensive Pirarie Scarsly a tree to be Seen but as We prograss We
find Sign of Buffelow We See some deed and Some Caberey[28]—
in the Evening on our left We Seen Ward one of our men on Hors
back Running a buffelow Some of [us] put off to asist Him but He
killed the large Buffelow Bull before We over took Him—after
takeing What meet We Wanted—We Went on makeing 23 miles and
Camped on a River about 50 yds Wide Running West Soposed to be
the Bad Salean[29]—the Watter is Clear and deep at this place Some
Sign of Bever our Corse this day is North 60 West—

the Pirarie threw Which We passed this day is nearly leavel With
a Rich Black Sandey Soil there is no other Rock Except that of
limestone Which only appeer in Spott on the Sides of Branches and
on the top of Some of the Highest ground—for there is no Hills
Heare there is Some timber along the branches

5th We Set out Early Crossing the River a little below our
october Camp Wheare there is a good ford and at about two miles
1821 Crossed a large Crick 100 feet Wide it Corse South East
and about 10 miles Crosed a Crick 50 feet Wide all So
Running South East Heare the Pirarie is a little more Roleing—
and at 18 miles Crosed a crick—and 19 miles inCamped[30] on a
Crick the West forke of the Same the meet Below Wheare We
Crosed—Heare the Cuntry Still Continues to be a little Roleing the

[28] Cabree or cabri—the American antelope, *Antilocapra americana*.
[Becknell had seen these animals about a month earlier. He called them
"goats," and added, "They were so sharp sighted and wild we could not shoot
them." William Becknell, "Journal of Two Expeditions from Boone's Lick to
Santa Fé, by Capt. Thomas Becknell," in *Southwest on the Turquoise Trail: The
First Diaries on the Road to Santa Fe*, ed. Archer Butler Hulbert (Colorado
Springs: Stewart Commission of Colorado College and Denver Public Library,
1933), p. 57.]
[29] *Read* Bad Saline. But this is a mistake; the Saline or Salt fork of the
Arkansaw is far from here, on the other side of the main river. Qu: is the supposed "Bad Salean" a headwater of Buck Creek?
[30] Four questionable streams passed to-day; I suppose them to be the Beaver
creek and its tributaries already mentioned, as Fowler must cross these to strike
the Arkansaw at the only point which renders intelligible his itinerary up this
river to the Little Arkansaw at Wichita, Kas., as given beyond. Fowler appears to
be camped on Little Beaver creek, above its junction with Beaver creek; if so, he
is in the Kansas Indian Reservation, a few miles N. of present Kaw Agency.

land Rich the limestone appeers in some places along the Bluffs
Which are not High or Steep   Hear We seen great nombers of
Poor Buffelow Bulls[31] and Blame our Hunters for not killing fat
Cowes When there is not one to be seen

5th october 1821 [continued]

for We Cold not tell them apart at So great a distance and it Was in
vain for our Hunters to tell us there Was no Cows among So many
Buffelow as We Cold See at all most any time   Corse this No 50
West 19 miles—

6th october 1821

We set out Early over Butifull High Pirarie leavel and Rich and at
Eight miles West We fell on the arkensaw River[32] Hcare there is
plenty of timber all a long the River on both Sides as far as We Cold
See We are now out of meet and Blameing our Hunters for not
finding Buffelow Cows   the Have neglected to kill the Bulls When
the Cold and the are not so plenty as the Ware and We beleve Have
been latly drove off by the Indeans[33] as the are now shy.

6th octor 1821 [continued]

We now steered north leaveing the [Arkansaw] River on our lefft

31 ["The cows remain fat from July to the latter part of December. The rutting
season occurs toward the latter part of July, and continues until the beginning of
September, after which month the cows separate from the bulls, in distinct herds,
and bring forth their calves in April" (James, "An account of an expedition,"
XV, 247). See also Edward Douglas Branch, The Hunting of the Buffalo (Lincoln:
University of Nebraska Press, 1962), pp. 6–7.

If Fowler did not remember the relative qualities of cow and bull buffalo from
his own early experience in hunting them in Kentucky, he may have recalled
Pike's evaluation (Donald Jackson, ed., The Journals of Zebulon Montgomery
Pike [2 vols.; Norman: University of Oklahoma Press, 1966], I, 343). Probably
the hunters themselves already knew.]

32 At a point somewhere within the present Kansas Indian Reservation, in
Oklahoma, perhaps not far from opposite the mouth of Chilocco or Chilocky
creek, a little S. of the Cherokee strip.

[Following Coues's identification of the route and camp sites, this camp was on
the small Kansas, or Kaw, Reservation, which in 1890 was bounded on the north
by the line between Indian Territory and Kansas, and on the west by the Arkansas
River. The area comprises the portion of Kay County, Oklahoma, lying east of
the Arkansas.]

33 [These Indians had probably come from the deserted Osage village the party
had visited on September 29. They may have been searching for their enemies, the
Cherokees, or they may have been following the same route Glenn and Fowler
were taking to the buffalo country in the vicinity of the Big Bend of the Arkansas
River. Carter, Territorial Papers, XIX, 320–57.]

Hand Beleveing the High Hill and Bluffs Near the River Wold be difequal to pass With loaded pack Horses—at 6 miles over High Rich lime stone Pirarie We Camped on a Crick [34] 60 feet Wide Wheare We killed Some turkeys in the Evening—We Ware all So informed by Some of the party that Indeans Ware Camped at no great distance—

7th october 1821   We moved West up along neare the [Arkansaw] River over Some High Rockey Bluffs and threw a large Sandy bottom to the bank of the River makeing five miles and Camped near the Indeans from them got Some dryed meet Corn Beens and dryed Pumkins for [which] We paid them In Such artickels as the wanted— these are the osage Indeans and the first We met With on our Route the [they are] frendly the Weather is now giting Cold With High Winds   Cloudey and Rained threw the night—the timber in the bottoms and Hill Sides is a king [kind] of Jack oak and very low Cotten Wood and Willow groes along the River—we stoped at this place for the purpose of purchasing Horses Haveing left two be Hind and three more unfitt for Survice makes us bad of for Horses and the prospect of provetions is not promesing as We Heare the Indeans are Camped for alonge Way a Head of us threw Wheare We must pass let [left] one Horse With an Indean—

8the october 1821

We moved up the River N 45 West two miles and Camped the Rain Still Continues Heare Conl glann purchased one Poor Hors at a High price and Highered one Indean to go along With us   Some of the Hands killed 10 turkeys

9th octr 1821—

We Set out Early and Steered north leaveing the River at Right angles over Riseing butifull Pirarie three miles to White River [35] about 70 yᵈˢ Wide Running West into the arkensaw this River Has a Continued grove of timber all alonge its Cores [course] as far as We

[34] Apparently the stream now known as Grouse creek, which traverses Cowley Co., Kas., on a general S. S. W. course, to fall into the Arkansaw in the Cherokee strip, between Kansas and Oklahoma.

[35] White or Whitewater is a former name of that stream which is now known as Walnut creek, and on which is situated Winfield, seat of Cowley Co., Kas. Its general course is S. through Butler and Cowley counties, but it loops both E. and W. on approaching the Arkansaw. Fowler says he struck it on its W. bend, which is above the place called Arkansas City, and if, after crossing it, he ascended it for 8 m., he proceeded about N. W. in the direction of Winfield.

[The name Whitewater River is used for the chief western tributary of Walnut River.]

Cold see and the land Rich—We Crosed this River leaveing it on our Right and up it at Eight miles Camped on the South West Side for the purpos of purchasing Horses   Sucseeded in Swoing [swapping] two and purchasing two at a High price—the Indeans advise us to Cross the arkensaw and Steer West Corse[36] and strike the arkensaw at the big timber[37] Near the mountains but the Season is late and Want of Wood and Watter Renders it a Hazous undertakeing —the Indeans Say it is about two days travel to the little arkensaw— the Hunters Brought in four deer one very fine Buck the first good meet We Have Head the land on this Creek is Rich and and Well timbered along the bottoms the Bluffs furnis abundance of lime Stone for all purposes of Building and fenceing— and is Capeable of makeing one of the finest Settlements in the united States—there being a nomber of the best of Springs

10th octr 1821

We purchased yesterday one small Hors and one to day—But when We gethered up our Horses to move off Robert Fowlers Horse Was mising—all tho He Was With the Rest in the morning— We Conclude the Indeans Have Hiden Him in the Woods and leave Peno to Sarch for Him and to fetch up Barbo left Sick With Him— all so left a Blanket to give the Indean that find or Return the Horse

11th octr 1821

We Set out Early leaveing [Walnut Creek] on the Wright and Steering N 25 West fifteen miles over High Pirarie to a small Crick and Camped[38] Near its mouth yesterday Peno Returned With the

36 [The decision to follow the Arkansas River around the Big Bend instead of cutting across country to the west was a realistic one. Although the expedition might have saved a few days' time by heading directly west, the men were in no great hurry and the shorter course, without wood or water, would have been hazardous.]

37 [The Big Timbers on the Arkansas River was called Tall Timbers by the Indians and was also known as The Grove. It is thought that before white men came to the country the trees extended from Big Sand Creek thirty miles up the Arkansas to the mouth of Caddoa Creek. Buffalo were plentiful in this area during the winter, and it was in consequence a favorite camping place for the Indians. George Bird Grinnell, "Bent's Old Fort and its Builders," *Kansas Historical Collections*, XV (1919–22), 28–91; and Clyde Porter and Mae Reed Porter, collectors, *Matt Field on the Santa Fe Trail*, ed. John E. Sunder (Norman: University of Oklahoma Press, 1960), pp. 140–41.]

38 Nearly on the line between Cowley and Sumner counties, Kas.

Sick man but With out the lost Hors the Hors is no doupt Stolen and With the knoledge of the Chiefs. these last Indeans appeer more unfriendly and talk Sasy and bad to us but this Is to be Exspected as the Come from the upper vilege and are Said to be a Collection of the Raskals from the other vileges

12th october 1821

Cloudey and Rains a little We Set out Early North 60 West fifteen miles over a Rich low Ridge there is Scarcly a tree or a Stone to be Seen and Hole land Covered With tall grass there is all along Whight River and on this Ridge much sign of Buffelow but the Indeans Have drove them off—We Camped on Small Branch[39] Near the arkensaw River

13th octor 1821

We Set out Early up the River Leaveing it on our left at a Bout 14 miles   Crossed a Small Crick on which is a large Beed of the Plaster of Paris at 20 miles We Camped on the Bank of the little arkensaw[40]—one Indean Cheef and two young me[n] viseted us at Camp and stated the Ware [they were] glad to see us Whitemen and frends—as they Had Seen or Heared Some of our men Last Evening and Soposed them be Paneys [Pawnees][41] and their Enemies on

[39] Vicinity of Mulvane, on or near the line between Sumner and Sedgwick counties, Kas.

[40] At Wichita, seat of Sedgwick Co., Kas., where the Little Arkansaw joins the Arkansaw river.

[The Osage Indians who hunted in this area called the stream Ne Shutsa Shinka, "the young or little red water." The Santa Fe Trail later crossed its headwaters near their source. At one time the stream was the dividing line between the range of the "reservation" Indians to the east and the "wild" Indians, whom the Osages called Paducas, to the west. About six miles above its mouth was the western end of the great hunters' trail from the Verdigris and Neosho rivers far to the southeast. On the map of Le Page du Pratz, *Histoire de la Louisiane*, I, 138, the junction of the two rivers is marked Mine d'Or. In 1836, Jesse Chisholm explored the area in search of the gold mine but failed to find it. Here in 1843 the John McDaniel party from Missouri captured Don Antonio José Chavez, traveling toward Missouri with a wagon train, and murdered him. In 1858 an Indian trading post existed near the stream. James R. Mead, "The Little Arkansas," *Kansas Historical Collections*, X (1907–1908), 7–14; and William R. Bernard, "Westport and the Santa Fe Trade," *ibid.*, IX (1905–1906), 552–65.]

[41] [According to Marquette, the Pawnees lived on the Red River at a place he recorded on his map as "Paniassa." From that area they migrated northward, near the Rocky Mountains, until they reached the country drained by the Kansas River and its tributaries. There Coronado, the first European they had contact

which acoumpt the Head [they had] all left their Camp and Hid them Selves in the timberd lands on the River—

14th oct 1821

We Set out Early Crossing the little arkensaw and steering West at 12 miles Came to the Banks of the arkensaw thence up the River North 70 West   We Camped on the [left] Bank [42] With out trees— We yester left one Horse   He gave out—and this morning discharged the Hiered Indean—the Cuntry Continues fine the land leavel and Rich the timber is plenty on the little arkensaw and Some for a few miles up the main River but Heare there is no timber or Willowes on the River Buffelow Bulls still appeer But no Cows and we are now Satisfyed of the Caus of the Hunters not killing any of that Speces no Sign of deer. tho We seen some turkeys last Evening

15the octobr 1821

We set out at our ushal time up the River No 80 West and Stoped at the mouth of a bold sreem of Watter 70 feet Wide [43]—but We Ware Soon alarmed by the Hunters Comming and Haveing Some Indeans on Hors Back and soposed to be in pursute of them—We Emedetly move up the River Crossing the Crick to some Sand Knobs on the River Bank about 400 yds above the mouth of the Crick—there being no timber We maid a Brest Worke of our Bagage and Remained the balence of the [day] Waiting the arivel of the Indeans—but none appeered—Some Buffelow Bulls Ware killed to day   We kept the Horses tyed up all night—yesterday the Sand Knobs appeer at about ten miles distance on our Right Hand and run Perellel With the River

Some Scatering trees appeer on the Knobs—

---

with, found them in 1541. When Don Juan de Onate visited members of the tribe in 1601 they had moved to the Platte River. Between that date and 1720, when they destroyed the expedition of Don Pedro de Villasur, they had occupied a wide region within the Platte basin. Lieutenant Zebulon Montgomery Pike found the Indians there in 1806. John B. Dunbar, "The White Man's Foot in Kansas," *Kansas Historical Collections*, X (1907–1908), 54–98; Frederick Webb Hodge, ed., *Handbook of American Indians North of Mexico*, Bureau of American Ethnology Bulletin No. 30 (2 parts; Washington: Government Printing Office, 1907, 1910), s.v. "Pawnee"; and Jackson, *Journals of Zebulon Montgomery Pike, passim.*]

[42] Up which the party will continue for many days. Camp to-day in Sedgwick Co., near the border of Reno Co.

[43] Cow creek, a considerable tributary of the Arkansaw, falling in below Hutchinson, seat of Reno Co. See Pike, ed. of 1893, p. 424.

16th october 1821

We Set out Early and maid ten miles up the River the Sand Knobs still on the Right We Sent out Some Hunters to kill a Cow but the Remained out all night We Ware much alarmed for their safety—no mee meet for Suppe or Brackfest—our Corse No 70 West and Camped on the River [44]

17th octr 1821

We Continued up the River North 65 West 15 miles and Camped on the Bank Scarcly a tree to be Seen—We this day pased the Head Spring [45] of the Crick at the mouth of Which We Camped on the 15th this [is] a large butifull Spring about three miles from the River on the north Side and in a leavel Rich Pirarie the Sand Hills appeer all a long on the South Side and near the River—the are not more then 60 or 70 feet High and the Cuntry leavel beyound them to a great distance those on the north about the Same Hight and Several miles from the River [46]—Which is from two to 400 yds Wide—With large Sand bars and low Islands this is its general Carecter as fare as We Have seen it

18th octr 1821

We Set out at our ushal time at ten miles pased a point of Rocks and a Hoop wood tree on them—to our Right and almost one mile from the River—and at [illegible] there is Some Cotten Wood trees along the River—at 18 miles We Camped [47] on the Bank Without

[44] At or near Hutchinson, Reno Co.

[45] The ultimate sources of Cow creek, at the mouth of which Fowler camped on the 15th, are of course afar off. He means a source of Bull creek, that branch of Cow creek which arises in the vicinity of Sterling, Rice Co., and runs approx. parallel with the Arkansaw past Nickerson, Reno Co., to join Cow creek a few miles below the latter place.

[46] The 1700-feet contour line is quite near the S. side of the Arkansaw for several miles along here, and crosses the river a little below Raymond, Rice Co., while on the N. side the same contour line is as far off as Lyons—some 11 or 12 miles. Fowler viewed the topography correctly.

[47] At or near Ellinwood, Barton Co. See Pike, ed. of 1895, p. 425. Fowler is fairly on the great bend of the Arkansaw, but not yet at the place called Great Bend.

[Though the travelers did not know it, they here intercepted the trail Coronado had followed across the Great Plains 280 years earlier. In this vicinity Lieutenant Pike reached the Arkansas River and camped for ten days, October 18–28, 1806. Stephen Harding Hart and Archer Butler Hulbert, eds., *Zebulon Pike's Arkansaw*

trees—Some Islands in the River the Higher grounds aproch nigher the River but Loos the appeeren of Sand Hills on the north

19th octr 1821

We set out at the ushal time and at 8 miles West We pased a point of Red Rocks about 600 yds from the River and at Eleven miles Crosed the paney River[48] about one and a Half miles above its

Journal (Denver: Stewart Commission of Colorado College and Denver Public Library, 1932), pp. 98–105; and Jackson, Journals of Zebulon Montgomery Pike, I, 336–40.

For information about Coronado's discovery see Jacob V. Brower, Quivira (St. Paul: H. L. Collins, 1898); Frederick Webb Hodge, "Coronado's March to Quivira," in Jacob V. Brower, Harahey (St. Paul: H. L. Collins, 1899); and Hodge, Journey of Coronado (San Francisco: Grabhorn Press, 1933), p. 112. Hodge located the point of discovery near Ford, in Ford County, Kansas, and proposed that Coronado continued downstream to Great Bend, in Barton County. See also George P. Hammond and Agapito Rey, eds., Narratives of the Coronado Expedition (Albuquerque: University of New Mexico Press, 1940), pp. 241–43, 291–92, 303–4.]

[48] A mistake—Fowler has not yet reached the Pawnee fork of the Arkansaw. His "paney River" is Walnut creek, near which is Great Bend, seat of Barton Co. This identification is proven by: (1) The west course assigned for to-day, the reach from Ellinwood to Great Bend being the only one in that direction. (2) The walnut and other trees named as growing on this stream. (3) The statement that this is the second stream crossed since leaving the Little Arkansaw—the only other one being Cow creek of note 43. (4) The courses and distances given beyond for the identifiable streams crossed, namely: Pawnee fork, Coon creek, and Mulberry creek, all of which fetch out quite right, if the present adjustment be made, otherwise all wrong. It would be curious to know if this is simply a blunder of Fowler's, or if Walnut creek was once known as "paney river"; most likely the former, as I have never met with the present malidentification before. See Pike, ed. of 1895, p. 425.

Fowler rounds the great bend, past Great Bend, and camps, as he says, 9 m. short of the true Pawnee fork. It will be observed that he has no name but "Red Rock" for the subsequently and long famous Pawnee Rock, which now gives name to a station on the railroad, said to be 16 m. above Great Bend and 13 m. below Larned. It is said to have received its name from a fight there in May or June, 1826, when an expedition which Col. Ceran St. Vrain had fitted out was attacked by Pawnees, and Kit Carson, then a boy, killed his own mule by mistake for an Indian during a false alarm the night before. "Pawnee Rock is no longer conspicuous. Its material has been torn away both by the railroad and the settlers in the vicinity, to build foundations for water-tanks, in the one instance, and for the construction of their houses, barns, and sheds, in the other. Nothing remains of the once famous landmark, its site is occupied as a cattle

mouth this is a deep bold Streem 50 feet Wide of Running Watter Banks High and about 80 feet Wide at the top Heare is ash Walnut Elm and Cottenwood over to this place Was West—this is the Second Streem We Have Crosed Since pasing the little arkensaw—We found a good ford [across Walnut Creek][49] and Steered South 50

---

corral by the owner of the claim in which it is situated," says Inman, Old Santa Fé Trail, 1897, pp. 404, 405.

[Pawnee Rock was one of the best-known landmarks on the Santa Fe Trail, and innumerable tales were woven around it (Edwin Legrand Sabin, *Kit Carson Days* [2 vols.; New York: Press of the Pioneers, 1935], I, 73). In addition to the story told by Coues (for which no source has been identified), another was told by Matt Field in his *New Orleans Picayune* articles in November 1840 (Porter and Porter, *Matt Field on the Santa Fe Trail*, pp. 99–104). Perhaps the best-known story is one given to Josiah Gregg. He had observed the rock in 1831 and wrote in 1843 that Pawnee Rock was "so called, it is said, on account of a battle's having once been fought hard by, between the Pawnees and some other tribe" (Josiah Gregg, *Commerce of the Prairies*, ed. Max L. Moorhead [Norman: University of Oklahoma Press, 1954], p. 42). Gregg's book was first published in July 1844. Perhaps the story he heard was the basis for Captain Cooke's lurid account. Cooke had an escort command on the Santa Fe Trail in 1843, and later wrote that the name of the rock

came from a siege there . . . of a small party of Pawnees by the Camanche hordes; the rocky mound was impregnable; but alas for valor! they were parched for thirst, and the shining river glided in their sight through green meadows! They drank their horses' blood, and vowed to the Wah-condah that their fates should be one. Death before slavery! Finally, in a desperate effort to cut their way to liberty, they all met heroic death; ushering their spirits with defiant shouts to the very threshold of the happy hunting grounds! The Camanches, after their melancholy success, were full of admiration, and erected on the summit a small pyramid which we see to this day. (Philip St. George Cooke, *Scenes and Adventures in the Army: Or, a Romance of Military Life* [Philadelphia, 1859], p. 259)

Joseph C. Brown had earlier mentioned the landmark simply as "Rock Point." "Field Notes of Joseph C. Brown, United States Surveying Expedition, 1825–1827," in Hulbert, *Southwest on the Turquoise Trail*, p. 117.]

[49] [Walnut Creek rises in Lane County, Kansas, flows almost due east, and enters the Arkansas River at the top of the Big Bend. Timber, principally ash and elm, was more plentiful there than at any other place west of Council Grove. Fort Zarah, two miles east of the modern town of Great Bend, near the mouth of the creek, was established in 1864 by General Samuel R. Curtis and named for his son, Major H. Zarah Curtis, who had been killed at Baxter Springs, Kansas, in 1863. The fort was built of sandstone quarried from nearby bluffs. It was abandoned in 1869, and settlers hauled the stone away. "Explanation of Map," *Kansas Historical Collections*, IX (1905–1906), 566.]

West Six miles to the Bank of the River—the land leavel as fare as the Eye Can see. Some Cottenwood on the Banks and Some Bushis. the Red Rock is evidently a volcanic production is porous like pomestone but heavier than common Sand stone—Back from the river 5 miles the Hunters reports very Large quantities of pomestone on the side of a hill which appears to them to be half blown off (Hill) by some cause—The sand and gravel thrown up by the Prarie Squarrels [*Cynomys ludovicianus*] [50] is precisely the same of that in the river for 5 or 8 miles distance from the river See great nombers of buffelow and Elks one of the Hunters killed three Cows but Haveing no Horse With Him the meet Was left out and lost Except a few pounds He Carryed in on His back—

20th october 1821

We Steered South 40 West and at nine miles Crosed a Crick [51] 40 feet Wide a bold Running streem about one futt deep and a few trees up it In sight. at ten miles We Camped on the River Bank in a low Bottom—at about three miles the ground Rises a little So as to form low Hills large Hords of Buffelow In Sight the Sand Hills Still appeer on the South Side of the River and to appeerence distetute of vigetation as the are Bald While those on the north are a Hard Black Soil With Some progecting Rocks and Covered With

[50] [The common prairie dog, a ground squirrel, was found over much of the Great Plains. It is very prolific, and colonies or "towns" twenty and thirty miles in length have been reported. Lieutenant Pike saw this village on October 24, 1806, and described it in detail. He wrote that the Indians called the little brown animals "wishtonwish" (Hart and Hulbert, *Zebulon Pike's Arkansaw Journal*, pp. 100–104; Jackson, *Journals of Zebulon Montgomery Pike*, I, 338–39; and Porter and Porter, *Matt Field on the Santa Fe Trail*, pp. 284–86). It was probably a part of this village, too, that Becknell had seen about September 28, 1821, and described as "a large settlement or town of prairie dogs, which appeared to cover a surface of ten acres." William Becknell, "Journal of Two Expeditions from Boone's Lick to Santa Fé," p. 58.

Major Long also described prairie dog villages. James, "An account of an expedition," XVI, 27–29.]

[51] *This* is the Pawnee fork, which Fowler crosses at Larned, Pawnee Co., and continues up the left bank of the Arkansaw. See Pike, ed. of 1895, p. 432.

[Fort Larned, seven miles above the junction of the Pawnee River with the Arkansas River, was established in 1859 for the protection of the Santa Fe trade. It was first called Camp Albert, but the name was changed in 1860 in honor of Colonel B. F. Larned, then paymaster general of the United States Army. Robert M. Wright, "Personal Reminiscences of Frontier Life in Southwest Kansas," *Kansas Historical Collections*, VII (1901–1902), 47–83.]

vigetation mostly a Short grass Something like Blew grass—on the
morning of the 18th Findley mounted his [horse] took With Him
His Blankets and Crossed the River to the South Side for the purpose
of killing a Boffelow Cow Since Which time We Have Heard nothing
of Him—yesterday morning Sent Back two men to look for Him—the
Have not Returned—We are afraid Findley is lost by going two fare
out in the Sand Hills We Exspect to Stop in about two days to Rest
our Horses and Wait for Findley to Come up—

21st Octr 1821

We set out at the ushal Hour and at Seven miles pased a point of
Rocks on Which stands two trees about 600 yds from the River—
and seven and a Half miles Came to a deep and mudey Crick[52]
100 feet Wide   Heare Some of our Horses Run to drink and Ware
Swomped With their loads and Ware forsed to be pulled out—We
Went [up] it about Half a mile and Crossed over and Camped about
three miles up it—Findley['s] mair gave out this day and Was left
We maid We maid ten miles this day South 50 West—this is a butifull
Running Streem With many fine Springs along its Banks—the
Hunters killed two Fatt Cows We Have now plenty of good meet—
the two men Returned but no word of Findley—a point of Hills or
Rocks appeers at seven miles distance near the River Bareing South
35 W—We gave this the name of Buffelow Crick[53] from one of our
Horses Being Swomped With the meet of a Buffelow on Him and
these anemels Being very plenty Heare

22nd octr 1821 monday

We Set out Early and at 7 miles pased the point mentioned
yester day a bout one from the River at fifteen miles Camped on the
Bank of the River about three miles to the left of our line of march
about 4 miles Back of our Camp We Crossed a Branch[54] of Bold

[52] Big Coon creek, which skirts the Arkansaw for a long distance, and on which
are Garfield, Pawnee Co., and Kinsley, Edwards Co. Camp in the vicinity of
Garfield. See Pike, ed. of 1895, pp. 434, 435.

[On more recent maps this stream is named Coon Creek.]

[53] The same Big Coon creek, up which Fowler is still going, approx. parallel
with the Arkansaw. Camp in the vicinity of Kinsley, Edwards Co.

[54] One of the forks of the same Big Coon creek.

[The expedition has now reached the lower end of that stretch of the Arkansas
known as Thousand Islands, which was mentioned in Hugh Glenn's trading
license. It extended upstream from a point just above Kinsley to Big Sandy
Creek, a distance of about two hundred miles. It was named for the numerous
islands in the stream.]

Running Watter 30 feet Wide—no timber Wheare We lay the men Waided over and geathered drift Wood for the night the Hunters killed one fatt Buffelow Some Cotten Wood on the South Side of the River above and below the Camp—the Sand Hills Still appeer on that Side the sand Hills aproch nier the River With Some Cotten Wood trees on them—Findley Returned

23rd octr 1821 tusday

We Set [out] at the ushal Hour South 10 West up the River maid ten miles and Camped in a low Bottom the Sand Hills Continue on the South—very leavel on the north for a great distance Back no timber on the north Side for the last two days march Emence Hords of Buffelow all traveling to the north While those we pased a few days ago Ware traveling to the South—We see maney Wild Horses— we Exspect [Indians are?] near us to the South Which moves the Buffelow to the north the Islands and sand bars still Continue But no bever We Head a fine feast last night on four fatt Buffelow Cowes

24th octr 1821 Wensday—

We Set out Early and at Seven miles the River Was 2½ miles to the left and at Eleven miles We maid the lower Eand of an Island on Which there is timber but none on Ither Side—the main Chanel is on the South Side Hear the High land aproch the River on both Sides— on the north Side there apperes a Whightis [whitish] Rock of Con- siderable Exstent the River makes Hear a Short Bend to the Right— the Cuntry Heare is a little Rolling But the land Rich and Butifull— no Wheare two steep for the Waggon or the plow. Heare at the uppe Eand of this Island the Bluff aproches the River and is the first above the little arkensaw—that that Shews it Rocky—on this Island there is good food for the Horses—and We Con Cluded to lay By one day to mend our mogesons and Rest our Horses as many of there Backs Ware Sore oing to the carelesness of the men the Horses are Poor and We Exspect that [some] of them Will not be able to Rech the mountains

25th octobr 1821

We Exspored the Cuntry for a few miles Round and on an Island about three miles above us found an Indean fort[55] Which might

55 [The Indian forts mentioned in the entries of October 25 and 26 were noticed by later travelers, none of whom records any more detailed information about them. The forts were apparently built by some of the Indians as protection against other Indians.]

Contain about 60 men this fort Is maid nearly Round and Built of logs layed on Each other—and is about two years old and must Have been built By a War party Which did not occupy it long—tho it Has been Inhabetid not more than two or three Weaks ago by Some People—the Haveing used fyer and left the Spit on Which the Head [they had] Roasted meet—above this Island a streem[56] of Bold Running Watter one Hundred and fity feet Wid puts in on the South Side—no timber at its mouth but timber appeers about two miles up it—its Cors is South 25 West—the Sand Hills Conting above this Crick but appers in a long Continued Ridge

26th october 1821 Friday

We Set out Early and Crossing the River to the South Side Steered our Corse West and Crossing the [Mulberry] Crick mentioned yesterday at six miles and Crossing a point of low land leaveing the River a bout 3 miles to the Right in the Bend and at twenty miles[57] Stoped on an Island Well Clothed With timber Heare Was all so an old Indean Fort Smaller than the other and Had been used by the Same pursons that Head lately been at the other We Heare Con Clude them to be White men[58] there Horses being

[56] Mulberry creek, falling into the right bank of the Arkansaw at town of Ford, Ford Co. Here is a case in which Fowler obviously reverses the course of a stream, giving the direction as it bears *from* himself; N. 25° E. is about right for Mulberry creek. See Pike, ed. of 1895, p. 436. This identification of Mulberry creek shows that we have fetched Fowler correctly from the great bend, his courses and distances proving to be near enough.

[It was in this area that Captain Philip St. George Cooke in 1843 captured and broke up Colonel Jacob Sniveley's Texas partisans who had marched up the Arkansas River to attack Mexican wagon trains on the Santa Fe Trail (William R. Bernard, "Westport and the Santa Fe Trade," pp. 553–56). At the mouth of Mulberry Creek was the "Lower Crossing" of the Arkansas River. On November 1, 1806, Pike had camped in this vicinity, either near Mulberry Creek or at a site five or six miles below its mouth. Hart and Hulbert, *Zebulon Pike's Arkansaw Journal*, pp. 112–13; and Jackson, *Journals of Zebulon Montgomery Pike*, I, 342.]

[57] The distance given sets Fowler at or near site of present Dodge City, seat of Ford Co., for many years the most notable point along this portion of the river, as it still is. See Pike, ed. of 1895, p. 437.

[Pike camped six or seven miles downstream from the site of Dodge City, Kansas, on the evening of November 2, 1806. Jackson, *Journals of Zebulon Montgomery Pike*, I, 342.]

[58] [Signs observed at this location and on the preceding day were the first indications that the Glenn-Fowler expedition had come upon the trail taken a short time earlier by William Becknell. On September 20, 1821, the Becknell

Shod—We Have as yet Head but three nights of frost and no Ice—
We Have not Seen one tree on Ither Side of the River the only apper
on the Islands and nothing there but Cotten Wood—at this Island
the main Chanel Is on the north Side

Satterday 27th octr 1821

We Set out Early Steering West [59] on the South Side of the River—
fifteen miles [60] to an Island the main Channel on the north Side—the

party had crossed the Osage River (i.e., the Marais des Cygnes) in Osage County,
Kansas. They seem to have been traveling very rapidly at first, for on the evening
of September 24 they reached the Arkansas River, probably near the northeastern
turn of the Great Bend. About September 26 they passed the site of Ellinwood,
which Glenn reached October 18 (see note 47), and the prairie dog town (see
note 50). They crossed a stream to which Becknell gave the name Hope Creek,
identified by Hulbert as Coon Creek, and the next day they crossed to the right
bank of the Arkansas River. The fort and camp site noted by Fowler on October
26 had probably been occupied by Becknell about October 2 or 3. The signs of
recent occupation Fowler reported on November 6 and 7 were probably evidence
of Becknell's camp about October 12. Hulbert, *Southwest on the Turquoise Trail*,
pp. 57–61.]

[59] [On this day's march, along the south side of the Arkansas River, they
passed the site of Dodge City and the 100th meridian, and thus they entered
Spanish territory.]

[60] Vicinity of Cimarron, Gray Co. See Pike, ed. of 1895, p. 438.

[The Cimarron, or Middle Crossing, was five miles west of Dodge City,
Kansas. In the fall of 1822, James Baird and Samuel Chambers, Spanish
prisoners with Robert McKnight from 1812 to 1821, set out from St. Louis for
New Mexico with a company of twenty men or more (perhaps as many as fifty)
and a train of sixty pack horses loaded with trading goods. They were caught in a
blizzard near this crossing and had to remain here through the entire winter.
The weather was so severe that nearly all their animals perished. In the spring of
1823 they dug pits in the side of a low hillock, where they stored their goods, and
went on to Taos. In New Mexico they secured new animals and then returned to
the Arkansas. After retrieving their buried goods they turned about once more
and traveled to Santa Fe. The pits, or caches, were among the most famous
landmarks on the Santa Fe Trail, and traces of them were evident for more than
a century. Louise Barry, comp., "Kansas before 1854," 523–24; Porter and
Porter, *Matt Field on the Santa Fe Trail*, pp. 56, 129; and Gregg, *Commerce of
the Prairies*, p. 47.

The trail beyond this crossing, later known as the Dry Route, the Water
Scrape, and the Cimarron Cut-off, ran southwest sixty-five miles across waterless
desert to the Cimarron River. On his second trip William Becknell took his
wagons across this route. Gregg, *Commerce of the Prairies*, pp. 14–15; Hart and
Hulbert, *Zebulon Pike's Arkansaw Journal*, pp. 112–14; Porter and Porter, *Matt
Field on the Santa Fe Trail*, pp. 71, 82 n, 288; and Sabin, *Kit Carson Days*, I,
19–21.

UNIVERSITY OF WINNIPEG
LIBRARY
515 Portage Avenue
Winnipeg, Manitoba R3B 2E9
DISCARDED

River as ushal is full of Islands With more or Less Cotten [wood] on them but none on Ither Side of the River—We this day left Findley With two Horses and one mule With Instruction to Remain on the Island five days and then to follow us as the Horses Wold be Rested by that time

28th octr 1821

We Set out at our ushal Hour and keeping up the River West ten miles [61] to a point of timber on the South Side the Rockey [hills] frequently appeer on the north Side and the Sand Hills on the South Some Scattering Cotten Wood trees gro on the Sand Hills one othe Hors gave out this day and Was left

monday 29th octr 1821

We Set out at our ushal Hour Steering N 70 West up the River at fifteen miles Crossed a Spring branch to a few Cotten Wood trees on the River Bank in low Bottom Where We Camped [62] for the night Heare the Hunters killed one deer and See Several more— this this the first We Have Seen Since We left the Paney River but the Buffelow and Elk are In great a bondance all the Way So that the Hunters kill [all] the[y] Wish We all So got two Cows to day— and See a great many Elk——

30th octobr 1821

We set out as ushal and Steered North 75 West ten miles to a low point of greavel and Sand Washed by the River the land Rises gently to the left for about one and a Half miles both above and below this point the Bottoms on the River are low—at fifteen miles We Camped [63] on an Island Clothed With tall grass and Cotten

---

Fort Mann was established at the Cimarron Crossing in 1847. It consisted of four log houses connected by woodwork with loopholes. It was about sixty feet across, with walls twenty feet high, and had two wooden gates, each one foot thick. The garrison comprised eleven men, none of them soldiers, and the commander was a civilian. Lewis H. Garrard, *Wah-To-Yah and the Taos Trail*, ed. Ralph P. Bieber (Glendale, Calif.: Arthur H. Clark, 1938), pp. 81, 330–39; and Robert M. Wright, "Reminiscences of Frontier Life in Southwest Kansas," *Kansas Historical Collections*, VII (1901–1902), 78.]

[61] Vicinity of Ingalls, Gray Co., or rather beyond.

[62] At some point beyond Pierceville, Finney Co. See Pike, ed. of 1895, p. 440. [Pike's camp on the evening of November 4, 1806, is identified "at about Pierceville." Jackson, *Journals of Zebulon Montgomery Pike*, I, 343.]

[63] Having passed Garden City, seat of Finney Co., by perhaps 8 or 10 m. [Pike "concluded to halt the day" November 5, 1806, at a camp "still in the general vicinity of Pierceville" (Jackson, *Journals of Zebulon Montgomery Pike*,

Wood trees—the main Chanel on the north Some Small Islands on the South With out trees

31st octr 1821 Wensday

We Continued our Rout on the South Side our Corse South Sixty five West [64] fifteen miles to a point of Woods on the River Bank   Heare is fine tall grass for our Horses and young Cotten Wood and Willowes are very plenty—a great many trees appeer to Have [been] Cut down by White men and a french trading Camp Have been latly burned down Soposed to [be] Shotoes [65] the Hunters

---

I, 343). His camp on November 6 is placed opposite or southwest of Garden City. Hart and Hulbert, *Zebulon Pike's Arkansaw Journal*, p. 115.

In this vicinity the Mallet brothers reached the Arkansas River on their way from Illinois to Santa Fe in 1739. They followed it upstream to the mouth of the Purgatory River, where they turned south toward Raton Pass and Taos. Henri Folmer, "The Mallet Expedition of 1739 through Nebraska, Kansas and Colorado to Santa Fe," *Colorado Magazine*, XVI (September 1939), 1–13.]

[64] This first southing seems to indicate a start from a point where the river reaches lat. 38° N., near the W. border of Finney Co., at about the distance last said beyond Garden City; whence the general course of the Arkansaw is nearly as said past Deerfield and Lakin to Hartland, Kearney Co. The distance given from this turn of the river would bring Fowler somewhere between the two last named places.

[65] Chouteau's, whose name was long borne by a large island in this vicinity, not easy to locate exactly. If there has been but one of this name, Chouteau's island has floated a good many miles up and down the river—at least, in books I have sought on the subject. Inman locates it near Cimarron, Kas., p. 42; at the mouth of Big Sandy creek, Col., p. 75; and his map agrees with the latter position. He says, pp. 40, 41: "As early as 1815, Auguste P. Chouteau and his partner, with a large number of trappers and hunters, went out to the valley of the upper Arkansas, ... The island on which Chouteau established his trading-post, and which bears his name even to this day, is in the Arkansas River on the boundary line of the United States and Mexico. ... While occupying the island, Chouteau and his old hunters were attacked by about three hundred Pawnees, whom they repulsed with the loss of thirty killed and wounded." (Auguste P. Chouteau, b. May 9, 1786, married Sophie A. Labadie Feb. 15, 1809; d. 1839. He was the eldest son of John Pierre Chouteau, and elder brother of Pierre Chouteau, jr., b. Jan. 19, 1789, d. Oct. 6, 1865.)

[This island was probably at the upper crossing of the Arkansas River, near the site of Hartland, Kansas. In the spring of 1816 the hunting and trapping party of August Pierre Chouteau and Jules de Mun, descending the river with their winter's catch of furs, was attacked by two hundred Pawnees, Otoes, and Rees. The men took refuge on the island, where they constructed ramparts with their packs. Although one man was killed and three were wounded, the party success-fully withstood the assault. When Major Bennett Riley with four companies of

killed this day three of the fatest Buffelows that Have yet Been Braught to Camp—Buffelow Elk deer Caberey and Wild Horses are in great nombers—High Wind all day—[66]

1st november 1821

Lay by to Rest Horses and dress Skins and prepare for Winter— this morning the first Ice We Seen frose in the Kittle about as thick as the Blaid of a knife and Ice floted down the River—the Bluffs or Hills on the north Sid aproch the River and those on the South are at about 3 miles distance—

2nd   Remained In Camp all day fine Weather—Some frost last night With Ice—

3rd November 1821

We Steered S° 65 W five miles to a low point of land With Rocks Washed By the River on thes Rocks are some Small Hoop Wood trees the first We Have Seen for a long time and those are the first Rocks We Have pased on the South Side of the River—Heare the [river] bends a little to the Right [67] We proceded ten miles further pasing Some fine Springs to the point of an Island on the South Side of the River Haveing pased over a point [of] bald Sand Hills Washed by the River about Half a mile below our Camp for We Camped on the lower Eand of the Island—Which is large and Well timbered With Cotten Wood—Heare We find the first fresh Sign of bever our Corse from the Hoop Wood trees to this place is N° 80 West—two of our Horses gave out this day and Ware left—on this Island the Hunters killed Some turkeys and Seen Some more. the first We Have Seen above the little arkensaw—the Wind Hard all day from the N—W—

4th Novr 1821 Sunday—

We Steered No 75 W four miles to [a point] of Sand Hills Washed by the River and at Six miles farther to an Island Clothed With

---

infantry was serving as the first military escort on the Santa Fe Trail in 1829, he made camp here and spent the summer fighting Indians. "Kansas Historical Markers," *Kansas Historical Quarterly*, X (November 1941), 344; and Otis E. Young, *The First Military Escort on the Santa Fe Trail, 1829* (Glendale, Calif.: Arthur H. Clark, 1952), pp. 18–29, 85–86.]

66 [Becknell reported for November 1 "a keen north west wind, accompanied with some snow." Hulbert, *Southwest on the Turquoise Trail*, p. 62.]

67 Exactly so—passing Hartland, seat of Kearney Co., and continuing 10 m. N. 80° W. to camp near border of Kearney and Hamilton counties, nearly in the position of Kendall, in the latter county. See Pike, ed. of 1895, p. 440.

Willow and Cotten Wood—the main Chanel on on the North Side of the Island the last 6 miles our Corse Was West [68]—and pased over one point of Sand Hills and one of gravle both Washed by the River Buffelow Scarce—two turkeys this day—our last nights In Campment appers the first Wintering ground We Have meet With. We pass Some old Camps and Some old tent poles—this day left the mule the [that] gave out a few days ago and Was braught up— [69]

5th novr 1821 Monday

We set out Early and Steered West five miles to a low point of land Washed by the River thence South 80 West and at foure miles [further] pased the beed of a large Crick [70] but no Watter or timber in sight the great quantitys of drift Wood all along its Banks and the Hunters [tell] us the See timber a few miles up it—at three miles farther makeing twelve miles this day   We Camped on an Island in

[68] Reading $4+6+6 = 16$ m. to-day, and the last course W., we should bring Fowler past Syracuse, seat of Hamilton Co., to the vicinity of Coolidge, and thus near the boundary between Kansas and Colorado. This lap seems to me to stretch somewhat, but such advance as I here indicate appears to be required to adjust Fowler's topography beyond, and bring him correctly to Purgatory river on the 13th. See Pike, ed. of 1895, p. 441. Compare also date of June 11, 1822, beyond.

[69] [In 1865, Fort Aubrey was established four miles east of the present town of Syracuse, Kansas. It was abandoned the next year. "A Survey of Historic Sites and Structures in Kansas," *Kansas Historical Quarterly*, XXIII (Summer 1957), 138.]

[70] Apparently that now known as Two Butte creek, from the S., falling in nearly opposite Wild Horse or Little Sandy creek from the N., a mile or two above Hollys, Prowers Co., Colorado. Camp 3 m. above Two Butte creek would be about 2 m. short of the station Adana, on the A. T. and S. F. R. R. See Pike, ed. of 1895, p. 442.

[In the summer of 1720, Lieutenant Pedro de Villasur set out from Santa Fe for the Pawnee villages on the North Platte. He passed through Taos, and, turning northeast, presently struck Two Butte Creek, which he followed down to the Arkansas River. The massacre of his forces on the night of August 12–13 near the confluence of the North and South Platte rivers was a heavy blow to Spanish influence among the western Plains Indians (Alfred B. Thomas, *After Coronado: Spanish Exploration Northeast of New Mexico, 1696–1727* [Norman: University of Oklahoma Press, 1935]). The fate of the Villasur expedition was no doubt known to Fowler from his reading of Pike's journal. Jackson, *Journals of Zebulon Montgomery Pike*, I, 325.

The Cheyennes called this place (at the mouth of Two Butte Creek) Piles of Driftwood, referring to the vast quantities of debris that had been swept down the stream in some unrecorded flood. George Bird Grinnell, *The Fighting Cheyennes* (Norman: University of Oklahoma Press, 1956), p. 65 n.]

the middle of the River—this Island is better Cloathed With timber Brush green grass for the Horses and grape vines than any We Have Seen Heare We found plenty of grapes that are good the first We Have met With in [this] part of the Cuntry the River Continu full of [islands] the one We are on is long and is a good Wintering ground Some Small Connues [canoes] may be maid Heare

6th novr 1821

determined to lay by on act of Wood and the Poor State of our Horses—We Have all Readey lost 13 Horses and two mules[71] and the Remainder Hardly fitt for use   We are Camped in a pawnee fort[72] Which appeers to Have been used about two Weakes Since— We Counted 11 tracks of Indians Barfooded in the Sand and found a Woolf that Head been Shott lying on the Sand Bare—

7th Novr 1821

We Set out as ushul and Steerd N° 80 West twelve miles[73] to a Small Island near the middle of the River We find this day that there is more gravle and less Sand in the River than below theres much more Watter and Cleareer than any Wheare below—the River is still full of Islands—vast Hords of Buffelow In Sight—no bever   We See old Sign of Indeans a great many Buffelow being killed in the Summer—We again See the Sign of White men a Head of us—[74]

[71] [The expedition has now lost half the pack animals with which it had started two months earlier. The losses were probably a result of overloading. A few replacements had been secured from the Indians near the beginning of the journey, but by this time every animal was carrying a double load.]

[72] [This was the third Indian fort Fowler had seen.]

[73] Past Adana, Granada, and Manville, to a point about opposite Carlton, Prowers Co.

[74] [For the three weeks from October 1 to October 21, William Becknell summarized his experiences in rather general terms:

We still continue meandering the Arkansas, but travel very slowly in consequence of the still continued ill health of some of the party. Our horses for the first time attempted to leave the encampment; and one strayed off which we never saw afterwards.

The water of the river is here clear, although the current is much more rapid than where we first struck it. Its bed has gradually become narrower, and its channel consequently deeper. The grass in the low lands is still verdant, but in the high prairie it is so short that a rattlesnake, of which there are vast numbers here, may be seen at the distance of fifty yards; they inhabit holes in the ground.

On the 15th we discovered a lake, which had every appearance of being strongly impregnated with saltpetre. Our horses having become very weak

8th november 1821 thorsday

We Set out as ushul our Corse N 85 W Crossing to the north Side of the River at three miles pased the Beed of a dry Crick[75] 75 yds Wide Corse [from the] north and only a few Scatering trees In Sight on it—at Six miles We Crossed the River on act of a Snow Storm to a grove of trees on an Island in the South Side and Camped for the night—this Island is formed by a large Crick[76] 80 yds Wide puting In on the South Side and a Slew of Watter Runing out of the River in to this Crick forming a large Island—there is timber In Sight up this Crick and large quantitey of drift Wood alonge it Banks—and from seeing the Same appeerence of drift Wood on other Cricks below Comeing from the South We Sopose there must [be] timber up those Streem as there is no drift Wood from the north—the River Banks are from 6 to 8 fitt High and the Watter much [more] plenty than below Buffelow Plenty and all traveling fast to the north—

9th novr 1821 Friday

Remained in Camp on acounpt of the Cold the Snow about ankel deep   Sent out the Hunters the killed 2 Buffelow Cows—the River is Heare deeper and Cruked and Points of [timber] in the bends more plenty—

10th Novr 1821

We Steered S° 65 West five miles to a point of timber on the South Side of the River Which is still narrow deep and Cruked it Bredth is from 150 to 200 yds Wide and deep a knof for Small Boats to asend—

11th novr 1821 Sunday

our Corse South 65 West at four miles pased a point of High

---

from fatigue and the unfitness of their food, we encamped three days to recruit them and dress some skins for moccasins; during which time we killed three goats and some other game.

On the 21st we arrived at the forks of the river, and took the course of the left hand one (William Becknell, "Journal of Two Expeditions from Boone's Lick to Santa Fé," pp. 60–61).]

[75] This large dry creek, from the N., is the Big Sandy, which falls in about the distance said above the camp which was on the island opposite Carlton. See Pike, ed. of 1895, p. 443. Somewhere about the mouth of Big Sandy creek is one of the locations of the shifty Chouteau's island mentioned in note 66.

[The expedition has now entered the upper Big Timbers.]

[76] Willow creek, on which is Lamar, seat of Prowers Co. See Pike, ed. of 1895, p. 443.

Rocks[77] about Half a mile South from the River from this Rock the Bluffs or Hills Continu to our left—and at Eight miles Camped at the mouth of a deep muddey Crick[78] Heare the Bluffs aproch the River on both Sides and are much Higher and Steep as Well as more Rockey than below—Heare is much old Sign of Indeans many Piles of Rock are Raised by them on the bluffs—one fatt Buck killed this day—there are some Bever Heare—

12th Novr 1821 monday

We set out Early and to Enable us to Cross the [Mud] Crick With the Horses We maid a Bridge of Brush and flags Which bore them over With Safty and Steered South 65 West Eight miles to the Point of a Ridge Bound With Rocks and Washed by the River—there is two mounds Covered With Rocks about 300 yds to the South of Camp and about Half a mile a part[79] We this day Crossed a Small [Caddoa] Crick at about four miles back from Camp—and pased over Several Ridges the points of Which Butted a gainst the River With progecting Rocks of the Sand Stone kind—the[re] We Seen Some Peaces of marble—the River Bottoms are about Half a mile Wide and and is offen Crosed from one Side to the other by the River Which is very Cruked and both Sides of the bottom or valley bound With the Bluffs and Rocks Buffelow plenty killed 3 Cows and one deer this day—

[77] [The "point of High Rocks" Fowler saw was a bluff about one mile north of Prowers, Colorado, on which William Bent built his stone fort in 1853. Four years later he leased it to the government as a storage place for Indian annuities. In September 1860, Major John Sedgwick, with four companies of the First Cavalry, built a new post on the north side of the Arkansas River about a mile west of Bent's New Fort and called it Fort Wise. In June 1862 the name was changed to Fort Lyon in honor of General Nathaniel Lyon, who had been killed in the battle of Wilson's Creek, near Springfield, Missouri, in August 1861. George A. Root, ed., "Extracts from Diary of Captain Lambert Bowman Wolf," *Kansas Historical Quarterly*, I (May 1932), 207–10; Grinnell, "Bent's Old Fort and its Builders," pp. 57–58; and David S. Lavender, *Bent's Fort* (Garden City, N.Y.: Doubleday, 1954), pp. 323–24.]

[78] Present name the same—Mud or Muddy creek, nearly halfway between Prowers, Bent Co., and Caddoa creek. See Pike, ed. of 1895, p. 443.

[79] A statement which serves to fix camp with perfect precision. The two mounds said are both between one and two miles due W. of Caddoa, and just the distance said W. of Caddoa creek. These isolated elevations appear in due form on the U. S. Geological Survey map of Colorado, Lamar sheet, near lower left-hand corner. The railroad cuts between the river and these bluffs, but the wagon road rises over them, back of their tops. See Pike, ed. of 1895, p. 443.

We this day Sopose We Seen the mountains for the first time tho We Have long looked for them the Hills or Bluffs on the North Side are High Being two bluffs one on the top of the other and about five miles apart [80]

13th novr 1821 tusday

Went to the Highest of the mounds near our Camp and took the bareing of the Soposed mountain Which Stud at north 80 West all So of the River Which is West We then proceded on 2½ miles to a Small Crick [81] Crosed it and asended a gradual Rise for about three miles to the Highest ground in the nibourhood—Wheare We Head a full vew of the mountains this must be the place Whare Pike first discovered the mountains   Heare I took the bareing of two that Ware the Highest [82] the longest South 71 W—the other Which

[80] Two special elevations across the river, directly in line from camp, are respectively 3975 and 4200 feet high, and their summits just about 5 m. apart.

[81] Present Rule creek, quite at the distance said from the twin bluffs at camp. [Pike reached Caddoa Creek ("Buffalo Creek"), Rule Creek ("Lookout Creek"), and the Purgatory River on November 15, 1806. Hart and Hulbert, *Zebulon Pike's Arkansaw Journal*, pp. 117–18; and Jackson, *Journals of Zebulon Montgomery Pike*, I, 345–46.]

[82] Las Cumbres Españolas—the celebrated Spanish Peaks. This is the place where, on the 15th of Nov., 1806, Pike's party gave "three cheers to the Mexican mountains." His map bears the legend: "Here the Mountains are first seen." It is a curious fact, now forgotten by most persons, that the Spanish Peaks were called and supposed to be Pike's Peak for some time—during the years that Pike's Peak was called James' Peak. Thus, Thomas J. Farnham, writing of 1839 in his Travels, New York, 1843, p. 41, says: "Pike's peak in the *south*west, and James' peak in the northwest, at sunset showed their hoary heads above the clouds that hung around them." Again, *ibid.*, p. 42: "Sixty miles east of these mountains [in Colorado and New Mexico], and 50 *south* of the Arkansas, stands, isolated on the plain, Pike's peak, and the lesser ones that cluster around it"—here also thus distinguishing it from James' Peak, north of the Arkansaw. As I have said in my edition of Pike, p. 457, where I discuss the first application of Pike's name to the peak which now bears it, the date has never been exactly ascertained; and here in Farnham we have the Spanish Peaks called by Pike's name so late as 1839. I suppose it will be difficult, if not impossible, to trace the proper appellation of Pike's Peak back of Frémont's expedition of 1843–44. At the time I penned my note on the subject I did not know that the misapplication of Pike's name to the Spanish Peaks had ever been current, and my reference to the verbal use of the term in the 30's may have had no other foundation. Pike's Peak having been first surmounted by Dr. Edwin James and his men, at 4 p. m., July 14, 1820, was formally named James' Peak in Long, ii, 1823, p. 45, from Long's MS. notes of July 15, 1820.

appeered like a point South 75 West—nither of those are the mountain Seen this morning—on looking forward We Seen a Branch Puting in from the South Side Which We Sopose to be Pikes first forke[83] and make for it—Crossed and Camped in a grove of Bushes and timber about two miles up it from the River We maid Eleven miles West this day[84]—We Stoped Heare about one oclock and Sent back for one Hors that Was not able to keep up—We Heare found some grapes among the brush—While Some Ware Hunting and others Cooking Some Picking grapes a gun Was fyered off and the Cry of a White Bare[85] Was Raised We Ware all armed in an Instent and Each man Run His own Cors to look for the desperet anemel— the Brush in Which We Camped Contained from 10 to 20 acors Into

---

[Here they passed the site of the second Fort Lyon, built in 1867–68 five miles below Boggsville, now the town of Las Animas, Colorado. Kit Carson died there on May 23, 1868.]

[83] Fowler's supposition is correct—this is Pike's "1st Fork" of the Arkansaw, Spanish Rio Purgatorio and Rio de las Animas Perdidas, French Rivière Purgatoire, English Purgatory river, often corrupted into Picket-wire, and also known as Las Animas river. It enters the Arkansaw from the S. in long. 103° 10′ W., midway between Fort Lyon (across the main stream) and the town of Las Animas, Bent Co. See Pike, ed. of 1895, p. 445.

Fowler names Purgatory river "White Bair crick" on June 6, 1822, beyond, from the tragic incident now about to be narrated.

[84] [Becknell wrote: "On the 21st [of October] we arrived at the forks of the river, and took the course of the left hand one. The cliffs became immensely high, and the aspect of the country is rugged, wild and dreary." Hulbert says that Becknell may have reached either the Purgatory River, or, a few miles farther west, the Timpas. "The former became the later stage-coach route; the latter, the route of the historic Santa Fe Trail. In either case the mountains reached were the Ratons" (William Becknell, "Journal of Two Expeditions from Boone's Lick to Santa Fé," p. 61). Becknell was twenty-two or twenty-three days ahead of Glenn and Fowler.]

[85] Grizzly bear, *Ursus horribilis*. Lewis Dawson may not have been the first American citizen to die and be buried in present Colorado, but I have found no such fact of earlier date.

[Hunters along the headwaters of the Arkansas, North Canadian, and Cimarron rivers sometimes encountered grizzly bears that had come down from the mountains in search of the carcasses of buffalo and elk. Dawson had probably never seen one of these ferocious animals when he made the fatal mistake of attacking and wounding this one while he was alone (Mathews, *The Osages*, pp. 454–55). Pike had described the grizzly bear, and Major Long had given even more detailed information. James, "An account of an expedition," XVI, 45–51. For information about the bears Pike shipped from New Orleans to Baltimore, see Jackson, *Journals of Zebulon Montgomery Pike*, II, 276, 278, 283–84, 292–94.]

Which the Bare Head [bear had] Run for Shelter find[ing] Him
Self Surrounded on all Sides—threw this Conl glann With four
others atemted to Run But the Bare being In their Way and lay
Close in the brush undiscovered till the Ware With in a few feet of it
—When it Sprung up and Caught Lewis doson and Pulled Him
down In an Instent   Conl glanns gun mised fyer or He Wold Have
Releved the man But a large Slut Which belongs to the Party
atacted the Bare With such fury that it left the man and persued Her
a few steps in Which time the man got up and Run a few steps but
Was overtaken by the bare When the Conl maid a second atempt to
shoot but His [gun] mised fyer again and the Slut as before Releved
the man Who Run as before—but Was Son again in the grasp of the
Bare Who Semed Intent on His distruction—the Conl again Run
Close up and as before His gun Wold not go off the Slut makeing
an other atack and Releveing the man—the Conl now be Came
alarmed lest the Bare Wold pusue Him and Run up Stooping
tree—and after Him the Wounded man and Was followed by the
Bare and thus the Ware all three up one tree—but a tree standing in
Rich [reach] the Conl steped on that and let the man and Bare pas
till the Bare Caught Him [Dawson] by one leg and drew Him back
wards down the tree. While this Was doing the Conl Sharpened His
flint Primed His gun and Shot the Bare down While pulling the man
by the leg be fore any of the party arived to Releve Him—but the
Bare Soon Rose again but Was Shot by several other [men] Wo
Head [who had] got up to the place of action—it Is to be Remarked
that the other three men With Him Run off—and the Brush Was so
thick that those on the out Side Ware Som time geting threw—

I Was my Self down the Crick below the brush and Heard the
dredfull Screems of man in the Clutches of the Bare—the yelping of
the Slut and the Hollowing of the men to Run in Run in the man
Will be killed and noing the distance So grate that I Cold not get
there in time to Save the man So that it Is much Easeer to Emagen
my feellings than discribe them but before I got to the place of action
the Bare Was killed and [I] met the Wounded man with Robert
Fowler and one or two more asisting Him to Camp Where His
Wounds Ware Examined—it appeers His Head Was In the Bares
mouth at least twice—and that When the monster give the Crush that
Was to mash the mans Head it being two large for the Span of His
mouth the Head Sliped out only the teeth Cutting the Skin to the

bone Where Ever the tuched it—so that the Skin of the Head Was Cut from about the Ears to the top in Several derections—all of Which Wounds Ware Sewed up as Well as Cold be don by men In our Situation Haveing no Surgen nor Surgical Instruments—the man Still Retained His under Standing but Said I am killed that I Heard my Skull Brake—but We Ware Willing to beleve He Was mistaken— as He Spoke Chearfully on the Subgect till In the after noon of the second day When He began to be Restless and Some What delereous —and on examening a Hole in the upper part of His Wright temple Which We beleved only Skin deep We found the Brains Workeing out—We then Soposed that He did Heare His Scull Brake He lived till a little before day on the third day after being Wounded—all Which time We lay at Camp and Buried Him as Well as our meens Wold admit Emedetely after the fattal axcident and Haveing done all We Cold for the Wounded man We turned our atention [to] the Bare and found Him a large fatt anemel We Skined Him but found the Smell of a polcat so Strong that We Cold not Eat the meat—on examening His mouth We found that three of His teeth Ware broken off near the gums Which We Sopose Was the Caus of His not killing the man at the first Bite—and the one not Broke to be the Caus of the Hole in the Right [temple] Which killed the man at last— the Hunters killed two deer Cased the Skins for Baggs We dryed out the Bares oil and Caryed it with us the Skin Was all so taken Care of—

14th novembr 1821

We lay in Camp takeing Care of the Wounded man and takeing the Bareing of the the three principle points of the mountains [86] as the appeer—

the first mountain or grand Peek Bares N 75 W—

the Second South 75 No W

South Eand of same S° 75 W

[86] The first of these is Pike's Peak; the second and third are the two Spanish Peaks. Besides the names of these latter which I have noted in note 82, they have also been known as Las Dos Hermanas—The Two Sisters; and when I was in that country I sometimes heard the French names Les Tetons and Les Mamelles. The Ute Indian name, Wahtoyah, meaning Twins, is taken by Lewis H. Garrard as the major title of his book, otherwise The Taos Trail, etc., Cincinnati, 1850—a boyish piece of work, but the readable work of a very bright boy, who has much to say from personal observation of Taos, whither Fowler is bound. He is well worth looking up in the present connection.

3rd mountain S° 70 W—

South Eand S° 69 W—

there is on this forke a Continuation of timber and Brush the princeple trees are Cotten Wood With Some Boxelder and Some Small Black locust

15th all posible Care Was taken of the Wounded man for Which purpose We lay in Camp

16th the unfortnet man died at day Brake—and Was Berred near the Bank With a Strong Pen of logs over Him to prevent the Bares or Wolves from Scraching Him up—this Is the [first] anemel of the kind We Have met With—

Heare Conl glann Haveing the Command of the party acted as the adminestrater and ordered the dead mans property Sold to the Highest bidder—and Was Sold as followes one Short Riffel and papetis [?]

to george Duglass	$15.00
one muskets Barrl } to Jacob Fowler }	5.00
one Blanket to } Eli Ward..... }	10.00
2 vest to pall a Blackman	2.00
Sundry small artickels } to dudley Maxwell }	175
	———
	$33 75

the Hole amting thirty three dollrs Which Each man Has to act [account] With Conl glann for What He purchased—

the timber on this fork is mostly Cotten Wood Some Boxelder and Some Small Black locust—the Bottoms are fine and large—With great droves of Elk and Buffelow and Sign of more of the White Bare—there are all So Wild Horses deer and Caberey the trees on the main River are Small but Some of those on the fork are large Enof to mak a Connue—the Watter In the fork is Sofecient to turn a large Sett [of] mills at this dry Season and Heare is timber for a Small Settlement—Stone In the Bluffs are In abondance for Building and fenceing—after Settleing all things We moved up the River South

73 West 12 miles [87] to a Small Bottom Covered With trees—on the South Side of the River—Haveing pased one Branch [88] at Six miles and one at nine miles boath on the north Side of the River—and opeset the first the River bore about Six miles to our Right—from our Camp Heare We took the bareing of the mountains—1st N° 72 W—2nd S 76 W 3rd S° 70 W—at this Camp on the Bluffs Was the appeerance of lead But We Head no time to Examen

[87] Vicinity of Robinson, about on the boundary between Bent and Otero counties, and near the site of Bent's fort, which was a noted place for many years. See Pike, ed. of 1895, pp. 446, 447, and to authorities there cited for description add Farnham, Travels, 1843, chap. iv, beginning p. 34. Fort William was an alternative name of the same establishment—so called after one of the Canadian-French Bent brothers, who were William, George, Robert, and Charles. In 1826 three of them, with Ceran St. Vrain, built a rude stockade on the N. bank of the Arkansaw *above* Pueblo—perhaps halfway up to Cañon City. In 1828 they moved down below Pueblo, and began the erection of the permanent structure called Fort William, which was long better known as Bent's "old" Fort. It existed till 1852, when Col. Wm. Bent destroyed it with fire and gunpowder. He immediately selected a new site lower down the Arkansaw, on the same (N.) side, in the well-known locality of the Big Timbers, where he erected Bent's "new" fort in 1853, and used it as a trading-post till 1859, when it was leased to the Government; Col. Bent moving to a point just above Purgatory river for the winter of 1859–60. Next spring Bent's place became Fort Wise, so named for the Governor of Virginia, but in 1861 this name was changed to Fort Lyon, in honor of Gen. Nathaniel Lyon, who was killed at the battle of Wilson's creek, Mo., Aug. 10, 1861. In the spring of 1866 the river undermined this post, and it was moved to a point 20 m. lower down, though the old post continued to be used as a stage station by Barlow, Sanderson and Co.

[See note 77. Coues was mistaken here. Bent's stone trading post, located on a bluff (Fowler's "point of High Rocks") in the upper Big Timbers, was known from 1853 to 1862 simply as Bent's New Fort. Then the name was changed to Fort Lyon. On August 8, 1860, Captain Lambert Bowman Wolf recorded that Major John Sedgwick of the First Cavalry had been ordered to march four companies of that regiment to the vicinity of Bent's New Fort and establish a new post. In compliance with this order, Sedgwick chose a site on the river bottom near the Arkansas about a mile west of Bent's New Fort and began building Fort Wise on September 10. It was occupied until 1866, when erosion of the river bank threatened to destroy it. Fort Wise was abandoned, and in the same year Fort Lyon was moved up the river almost to the mouth of the Purgatory. Root, "Extracts from Diary of Captain Lambert Bowman Wolf," pp. 209–10; Lavender, *Bent's Fort*, p. 365; Porter and Porter, *Matt Field on the Santa Fe Trail*, pp. 72–73 n.; and Susan Shelby Magoffin, *Down the Santa Fe Trail and into Mexico*, ed. Stella M. Drumm (New Haven: Yale University Press, 1962), pp. 59–64.]

[88] Adobe and Horse creeks. See Pike, ed. of 1895, p. 446.

17th novr 1821 Satterday

I Went on South 5 miles to a High mound and took the Bareing of the mountains as followes 1st the grand Peek north 70 W—2nd not to be Seen 3rd S° 71 W 4th S° 49 W—our Corse from Camp up the River Was South 50 West twelve miles [89] to Whare the River Bends more to the West and Some deep gutters Washed down the Bank and the Hills aproch the River—thence S° 72 W. three miles to Wheare the River aproch the Hills again We pased one Small Crick at about 2 miles be low Camp and the other about Half mile the last about 30 yds Wide but no Watter Running and no timber In Sight— the River Bottoms are more narrow than for two days past—no Buffelow or turkeys there is Some deer and Sign of the White Bare one Hors gave out this day and Was left—the timber is more plenty in the Bottoms.

Sunday 18th Novr 1821

Continued up on the South Side of the River and at about two miles Crossed a dry Branch [90] and at foure miles a deep Branch [91] with Running Watter on Which there Ware several Bever dams With fresh sign of Bever the Branch about Eight Steps Wide at ten miles pased Close to a bend of the River and at Eighteen miles Camped [92] in a low Bottom and drove the Horses aCross the River for grass there being none on Wheare We Camped We find the Bottoms Widen from 4 to 8 miles the Hills much lower and the [ground] more leavle than for Several days past the Buffelow appers to Have left this section of the Cuntry as We Seen but one this day an old Bull With one leg Broken We Soposed by the Indeans—and that the Have drove the Buffelow all off—as their Sign is going to the South

19th nov 1821 monday

took the Bareing of the mountains from Camp this morning 1st north 67 W 2nd north Eand S 88 W South Eand S° 72 W 3rd S°

[89] At or near La Junta, seat of Otero Co., where the Arkansaw bends a little S. of lat. 38° N. See Pike, ed. of 1895, p. 447.

[90] Present Crooked creek, a little above La Junta. See Pike, ed. of 1895, p. 447.

[91] Timpas creek, about midway between La Junta and Rocky Ford, Otero Co. See Pike, ed. of 1895, p. 448.

[Pike's camp on the evening of November 17, 1806, was "at Timpas Creek, six miles southeast of Rocky Ford, Colo." Jackson, *Journals of Zebulon Montgomery Pike*, I, 346 n.]

[92] In the wide low bottom some 4 or 5 m. below Catlin, Otero Co., and about twice that distance short of the Apishapa river. See Pike, ed. of 1895, p. 448.

60 W—4th S° 39 W to the Highest Peek ther appeers a longe Ridge
to Contnue from the South and a Ridge Runs north from the High
Peeke—We Steered West up the River and at 10 miles Crosed a dry
forke[93] of the River 80 yds Wide but dry at present at fifteen miles
Camped in lott of woods on the River Bank Haveing at about 11
oclock Seen a large Smoke ahead and believing it proceded from the
Indeans fyer We Halted to look out for them—and in a few minets
two of our men Came in Company With one Indean—and in about
Half an Hour there Was between 30 and 50 Came Rideing at full
Speed With all their Weapons of [up] in a florish as tho the Ware
Chargeing uppon an Enemey but on their near aproch the most
frendly disposition appereed in all their actions as Well [as] gusters—
by this time We Hed Some meat Cooked of Which the Willingly
purtuck but Spareingly—as it after Wards appeered the Head
plenty at their Camp and Eat With [us] out of pure frendship—
amongst party Was the princeple Cheef of the Kiaways for these
Ware of that nation—the Cheef With three others Stayed With us
all night the others Returned to their Camp about Sundown[94]

[93] Apishapa river, now crossed by the railroad 4½ m. above the station Catlin,
already named. Camp said to be 5 m. above this river. See Pike, ed. of 1895, p.
448.
   [This camp was across the river and almost opposite the site of Fowler,
Colorado.]
   [94] [These were the first Indians the men of the expedition had seen since
October 15, five weeks earlier. They were Kiowas who, it may be supposed, had
completed their fall hunt and were now moving up the Arkansas to trade and
visit with other nations that had been hunting on the western Great Plains. The
men were now approaching the most dangerous region they would visit. From
November 22 to December 25 their very survival was more than once in
doubt.
   According to the oldest traditions, the Kiowas lived around the Three Forks of
the Missouri River, near the sites of Gallatin and Virginia City, Montana. They
divided into two bands, one of them moving to the northwest, the other to the
south. The latter band encountered the Crows, with whom they formed an
alliance and lived on cordial terms from about the beginning of the eighteenth
century. Presently they seem to have occupied the Black Hills country in the area
that is now southwestern South Dakota. Under pressure from the Cheyennes and
Arapahoes they next moved south until they reached the upper Arkansas River.
There they encountered the Comanches, who dominated the country from the
Arkansas far to the south. A war followed, at the conclusion of which, about
1795, the Kiowas and the Comanches formed a confederacy that continued for
more than a century. In 1805, Lewis and Clark heard that the Kiowas were living
between the North Platte and Niobrara rivers. Lewis said that they numbered
seven hundred, of whom two hundred were fighting men, and lived in seventy

20th novmbr 1821 tusday

Collected our Horses Early—by Which time a great nomber of the Indeans arived from Camp and moved up with [us] and crossed over the River Which Was fordable but the Watter Cold and the Ice Runing a little—our Horses Ware so loded that our men Ware all on futt but the Indeans took them behind them on their Horses and Carryed them over the River—from our Camp to the Indeans was about three miles West—95

Heare the Cheef gave up one of His lodges for the purpose of Store[ing] the goods—and took posesion and Charge of all our Horses 96 threw the Hole of this day the Indeans Continu to arive and

---

tipis on the North Platte. Lieutenant Pike in 1803 estimated that they numbered one thousand men, and reported that they had been forced westward into the mountains around the headwaters of the Platte and the Arkansas. By 1820, Major Long found them still farther to the south, wandering across the prairies between the Arkansas and the "Red" (Canadian) rivers with the Arapahoes and the Comanches. Apparently, Fowler and Glenn encounter the Kiowas during this last period of migration, moving among the Arapahoes, "Snakes," Cheyennes, Crows, Paducas, and "Ietans" (Comanches). The uncertainties in the relationships among these six or seven nations created a profound hazard for Glenn and his trappers. Their response to the danger is one of the main features of the journal during the next four weeks. James Mooney, "Calendar History of the Kiowa Indians," in *Seventeenth Annual Report of the Bureau of American Ethnology* . . . *1895–96* (2 parts; Washington: Government Printing Office, 1898), part 1, pp. 153, 155, 166–67, 171; and Hodge, *Handbook of American Indians North of Mexico*, s.v. "Kiowa."]

95 This Indian camp, of which we shall hear more, appears from the indications given to have been on the N. side of the Arkansaw, a little over the border of Otero Co, about half way between Fowler's last camp and Nepesta, Pueblo Co.

[It seems already to have become customary for the chief to take the trading goods of such visitors under his protection in his own tipi. Also, he had sent some of his young warriors to take their horses out to graze. According to Fowler's estimate of more than two hundred lodges, and his later estimate (November 27) of twelve to twenty persons in each, there were now twenty-four hundred to four thousand or more Indians around them.]

96 [Here the Indian method of working with white traders begins to unfold. The Kiowa chief, having seen that the Americans carried a supply of trading goods, assumed the responsibilities of sponsor, guardian, and middleman in the trading that would follow. He could expect to receive valuable presents for those services and would have a voice in fixing the value of the trader's goods in terms of what the Indians had to offer. The overnight visit of November 19–20 was more than an expression of friendship. The chief was interested in protecting the traders' goods and horses from his own tribesmen and in preventing the chief of another tribe from supplanting him.]

Set up their lodges—So that by night We Ware a large town Containing up Wards two Honderd Houses Well filled With men Wemon and Children—With a great nombr of dogs and Horses So that the Hole Cuntry to a great distance Was Coverd—this Scenes Was new to us and the more So after our long Jurney Seeing no persons but our Selves—the Indeans Ware frendly takeing us to the lodges of their great men[97] and all Ways Seting Some meat for us to Eat. tho Some times Boiled Corn Beens or mush Which arteckels the precured from the Spanyards

Wensday 21st nov 1821

lay in Camp all day Eating and Smokeing With the Indeans—and took the Bareing of the mountains from a point one Half mile north of our Camp—High Peak N 61 W South Eand of Same mountain N 82 W Heare a new mountain appeers or is a Ridge in the forkes of the River North Eand N° 84 W South Eand N 87 W—N° 2 of the first mountains North Eand S° 87 W Highest Point S° 45 W—Heare the mountain takes a more Westwardly Corse and Continues a broken Ridge to a High point or Ridge and Stands S° 42 W—and falling a little lower and Continues to the forth mountains or double Peekes—Which Stands thus 4th S° 27 W 5th S° 25 West from this point We See no more of the mountains to the South   We See large parteys of Indeans Comeing in threw the day and Seting up their Houses or lodges—

22nd nov 1821—

Remained in Camp all day Holding Counsels Eating and Smokeing and traiding a little With Indans—

the snow Has now Increeced to about 10 Inches deep and the Wind Extreemly Cold the River frosen up Close the Ice to a great thickness—and Heare in the Coldest mornings you might see Several Hundred Children Naked—Running and playin on the Ice—Without the least appeerence of Suffering from the Cold—the Highatans[98]

[97] [The purpose of these councils was to enable the Indians to become better acquainted with the traders and to examine and appraise the trading goods.]

[98] Ietans—Comanches.

[Fowler has now recognized two Indian nations and identified them by name, the Kiowas and the Ietans. The next day he distinguishes a third and names them the Arapahoes. That evening (in the entry for November 24) he identifies five or six nations by name: "Ietans—Arrapohoes—Kiawa Padduce—Cheans—Snakes." Since he had been "Counting them over," he no doubt had recognized

amounting to about 350 lodges arived this day and Camped With the others We are now Incresed to a cettey—

friday 23rd nov 1821—

this morning a Councel Was hild amongst the Cheefs of both the nations and Conl glann With his Interpreter Was Sent for—and Was told by the Ietan Cheef that the Ware Readey to Receve the goods in His Posesion that His father the Presedent Had Sent them—But When He Was told that there Was no Such goods He Became in a great Pashion and told the Conl that He Was a lyer and a theef and

distinctions and groupings among them himself. He probably got the names of the nations from the interpreter Baptiste Roy; other trappers in the party may also have contibuted some information. "Padoucah" or "Paduca" was the name given by various Siouan Indians to the Comanches. The "Snake" nation were not the Snake Indians of eastern Oregon, but probably either one of the bands of the Comanches or the Comanche nation as a whole. "Ietan" is a name of obscure origin which was applied variously by explorers and writers of the early nineteenth century to Shoshoni, Ute, and Comanche Indians. Mooney proposed that the meaning of any given writer be derived "according to the general context of the description." In the Fowler journal the meaning appears to be the equivalent of "Comanche"; and as Fowler names both "Ietans" and "Snakes," the Snakes may have been a distinctive band of Comanches.

Grinnell in reading this journal understood the entry "Kiawa Padduce" to be the name of a single nation and proposed that it be identified with "Kiowa-Apaches," but just previously Fowler had written of the "Kiawas and Padducas" and probably regarded them as distinct.

Before historic times the Comanches, one of the southern tribes of the Shoshonean stock, are thought to have been living in southern Wyoming. Under pressure from the Sioux and other prairie nations they moved south. The Kiowas said that when they themselves moved south from the Black Hills, the Comanches were already living below the Arkansas. In 1719 the Comanches were mentioned as living in western Kansas. A century later (in 1805) they were reported to be roaming over the country around the headwaters of the Arkansas, Red, Trinity, and Brazos rivers in Colorado, Kansas, Oklahoma, and Texas. For nearly two centuries they were at war with the Spaniards of Mexico, and they carried out raids as far south as Durango. In 1820, Major Long found them on the prairies between the Arkansas and the Red and Canadian rivers. Hodge, *Handbook of American Indians North of Mexico*, s.v. "Comanche"; Walter P. Webb, *The Great Plains* (Boston: Ginn and Company, 1931), pp. 50–52; Grinnell, *The Fighting Cheyennes*, p. 38; Ernest Wallace and A. Adamson Hoebel, *The Comanches: Lords of the Southern Plains* (Norman: University of Oklahoma Press, 1952), pp. 6–16; Rupert Norval Richardson, *The Comanche Barrier to South Plains Settlement* (Glendale, Calif.: Arthur H. Clark, 1933); and Alfred B. Thomas, *The Plains Indians and New Mexico, 1751–1778* (Albuquerque: University of New Mexico Press, 1940), pp. 1–39.]

that He Head Stolen the goods from His farther[99] and that He the
Cheef—Wold take the goods and Segnefyed that He Wold kill the
Conl and His men too upon Which the Conl and His Inturpreter
With drew—the Cheefs of both nations Remaned in Counsel all day
—and our Setuation Was not of the most plesent nature. the Kiaways
Ware our frends But the others Ware the most numerous—the
former Clames us their property and frens But the later We aprehend
intend to use force and in this Setuation We Remained all day—the
young Warriors Crouded Round us so that We Cold Scarcly Stir—
about Sun down a tall Indean Came Runing threw the Camp
Calling out—me arapaho[100] Cheef White mans mine and Shakeing
Hands With us as fast as poseble asked for the White man Captain
and on being Shoon In a lodge Wheare Conl glann With the Inturpreter Was—He Rushed in—but Was out In an Instant thumping
His brest With His fist saying White man mine arapoho Plenty
Pointing the Way He Came—from [which] We soon understood that
the Hole nation Ware at Hand and that We Head nothing to dred
from the Highatans—Who began to disappeer from about us—and
from that time We felt In Purfect Securety Haveing two out of three
of the nation In our favour and part of the 3rd our frends—but the
are all Sobordenet to their Cheefs—

Satterday 24th november 1821

a nomber of Cheefs of other nations arive In Camp—thing Ware
[things wore] a better appeerence—We Sopose there Is now about
350 lodges[101]—Some little traid for Buffelow Roabs for the benefit
of the Hands on our arivel at this Camp there Was about forty

[99] James Monroe, then President of the United States.

[100] [The Arapahoes were Plains Indians of the Algonquian family who lived in
prehistoric times around the Red River valley of northern Minnesota, according
to their own traditions. Probably about the beginning of the eighteenth century
they moved southwest, crossed the Missouri River, and then continued to drift
south and west. Eventually they broke into two main bands, a northern division
at the edge of the Rocky Mountains around the head of the North Platte River,
and a southern division that moved on toward the Arkansas. The latter were
undoubtedly the tribe encountered here. Hodge, *Handbook of American Indians
North of Mexico*, s.v. "Arapaho"; Pierre Tabeau, *Narrative of Loisel's Expedition
to the Upper Missouri*, ed. Annie Heloise Abel (Norman: University of Oklahoma
Press, 1939), p. 98; Warren Angus Ferris, *Life in the Rocky Mountains, 1830–
1835* (Salt Lake City: Rocky Mountain Book Shop, [1940]), p. 312.]

[101] [According to Fowler's estimate, there were from forty-eight hundred to
eight thousand Indians camped around them that night.]

lodges of Indeans—Kiawas and Padducas the Continu to Increes and last night on Counting them over find now four Hunderd of the following nations—Ietans—Arrapohoes—Kiawa Padduce—Cheans [102]—Snakes [103]—the Ietan the most numerous and the most Disperete the Arrapohoes the Best and most Sivvel to the White men Habits—but Heare We find some difficulty in Councl With So many Indeans—and no Inturpreter But Mr Roy—He Spoke Some Pane and [in] that language our Councils Ware Held—the Indeans are Sartainly Ignorent of the Ways or Customs of the White man and Have less Capasety to larn then any Indeans I Have yet Seen—the Have many Wants but no meens of Supplying them—Haveing nothing to traid but Horses and them We do not Want—We have found amongest them about 20 Bever only the Early Habits of those Indeans Precludes them from makeing Bever Hunters as the Cuntry Which the In Habet Contains but few—and the Indeans Hunt the Buffelow

Sunday 25th novem 1821

We found Withe the Ietans a Spanish Prisnor [104] Whome With great difeculty We purchased yesterday With $150 in goods and He In Joyed one night of liberty a Hapey Chaing from that of a Slave to an Indean—but unfortnetly—at day light this morning the goods Ware Returned and the Prisnor taken back to His formor master again—but We Will Spair no means in our power [to] Releve Him again and Send Him out of their Reech this man is from the Southern

102 [In the middle and latter parts of the seventeenth century the Cheyennes lived in Minnesota. Later they moved into eastern North Dakota, and then, pressed by the Sioux, they continued westward toward the Missouri River. Presently they were in the Black Hills region of western South Dakota, where Lewis and Clark found them in 1804. During the next few years they moved constantly farther to the west and south. The movements of the Kiowas, Cheyennes, Arapahoes, and Comanches brought those nations into conflicts with each other that continued for many years. Hodge, *Handbook of American Indians North of Mexico*, s.v. "Cheyenne"; Grinnell, *The Fighting Cheyennes*, pp. 3–11, 35–44; and John Stands In Timber and Margot Liberty, *Cheyenne Memories* (New Haven: Yale University Press, 1967).]

103 [Sometimes the Comanches, or one tribe of the Comanches, were called Snakes.]

104 [On their raids into Mexico and the territory that later became Texas the Comanches not only stole horses but also carried off men, women, and children. The adults were enslaved, but the children were adopted into the tribe and reared as members of it.]

Provence near St Antoni [105] With Which the Indeans are at War—
tho at Peece With new maxeco and the Spanish in Habetance there—
We Have been viseted by Some of the Spanish Indeans from maxeco
the live in the vilege of Tows [106]—its Six days Easey travel from
Heare—the are all Catholicks the Indeans Inform us that there are
White men [107] near the great [Pike's] Peak of the mountain on the
River Platt—and three days Hard travel from this place—

on the night of the 23rd a Snow fell about one foot deep and the
Weather is now Cold the River frosen up the Ice a great thickness
and the Indean Children that is able to walk and up to tall boys are
out on the Ice by day light and all as naked as the Came to the
World Heare the are at all kinds of Sport Which their Setuation
Will admit and all tho the frost is very seveer the apper quite Warm
and a lively as I Heave Ever Seen Children In mid Summer I am
shure that We Have Seen more than one thousand of these Children
on the Ice at one time and Some that Ware too young to Walk Ware
taken by the larger ones and Soot on a pece of skin on the Ice and In
this Setuation kick its [legs] Round and Hollow and laff at those
Round it at play—I have no doupt but that to take one of our
White Children and Put it In Such Cold Weather in that Setuation it
Cold not live Half an Hour on the 23rd four Ietan Indeans arrive
With the news of Peace being maid With the osages by the Big
Cheefs below—

five days before our arival at this place a battle Was faught Near
the mountains betwen those Indeans and the Crows [108] in which the

[105] San Antonio, Tex.

[106] Pueblo de Taos, N. M.

[These Indians from the pueblo at Taos had presumably come to the upper
Arkansas to trade and to hunt buffalo.]

[107] [The white men have not been identified. They may have been French
traders who had gone up the Missouri River to the mouth of the Platte and
followed that stream to the Rocky Mountains.]

[108] [The Crow Indians were a Siouan tribe forming part of the Hidatsa group.
They separated from the Hidatsa about 1776 as a result of a division into two
approximately equal factions under rival chiefs. The Crows were then living
along the Missouri River. Following their separation they moved westward
toward the Rocky Mountains. At the time of the Lewis and Clark expedition
(1804) they lived chiefly along the Yellowstone. Their presence on the upper
Arkansas River illustrates their nomadic way of life. Hodge, *Handbook of
American Indians North of Mexico*, s.v. "Crows"; and Robert H. Lowie, *The
Crow Indians* (New York: Farrar and Rinehart, 1935).]

formor lost nine men and the latter fifteen—amongest the arrapohoes
In this Ingagement there Was one young Warear that about two
years ago Was Shot threw the boddey and all the Skin taken off His
Head down to His Ears for a scelp—and in the last battle Was Shot
threw one of His feet Which Is now getting Well—and on this
[occasion] an alarm Was Raised of a War party apoching Camp
When this man With His father Was amongst the foremost on Hors
back to meet danger—but the alarm Was With[out] foundation and
all Returned to Camp With[out] a fight

the Kiawa Cheef Reported to us that He Head ben In Council all
day on the 23rd With the Ietan Who proposed to Him to Join In a
War against osages and the White men—to Which He disagread—
dureing the Hole of that day the Ietan manefested a very unfriendly
dispsetion to Wards us—and the Princeple Cheefs Informed us that
When mager longe[109] Was there He told them that the Predesent
Wold Send them plenty of goods and that the goods We Head Ware
Sent to Him and that We Head no Wright to traid them but When
He discovered that His demands Wold not be Complyed With
Chainged His disposetion and Seems very frendly and this night
offered Conl glann and Mr Roy Each one of His Wifes—the greates
token of frendship those Indeans Can offer—but the offer Was de
Clined telling Him that it Was not the White mans Habits

26th nov 1821

We moved one mile down the River to take a better Camp and
Build a house and git of of being so Crouded—the Ietan and Some
of the Kiawa threatned to stop us but maid no atempt When We

[109] Major S. H. Long, whose expedition came down the Arkansaw and Canadian rivers in 1820. The "Predesent" above said is of course President Monroe.

[Major Long had taken his expedition west from Council Bluffs on June 6,
1820, and gone up the Platte River to the foot of the Rocky Mountains, where he
turned south. He reached the upper Arkansas on July 16. A few days later, near
the site of La Junta, Colorado, he decided to divide his men into two groups.
One, under the command of Captain John R. Bell, started down the Arkansas on
July 24. Long led the other and continued toward the south in search of the undiscovered source of the Red River. Captain Bell and his companions met Glenn
at Fort Smith on September 9. Major Long and the rest of the expedition
encountered Glenn between Fort Smith and the Verdigris trading post on September 12. They had mistakenly followed the Canadian River to the east; the Red
River lay still farther to the south. Fuller and Hafen, *Journal of Captain John R.
Bell*, pp. 269–80.]

Started. We maid our Camp With the old Kiawa Cheef Who moved along With us Heare We Have plenty of young Cotten Wood trees to Cut for the Horses—With good Setuation for our Camp—

27th nov 1821

Early this morning Was advised of thretned atack from the Ietan [110] and the Kiawa and Padduce Indeans in Consequnce of our moveing from their nibor Hood Set the hands at Work Cutting logs to build a House—a Report Came that the Ietans Had mounted Horses to atack us—We Continued at Work on a House—and Was Informed that a party to Protect us Head met the others and turned them back—the Arrapohos about day light this morning Commenced moveing to us and by night from two to three Hunderd lodges Ware Round us as Close as the Cold Set up their lodges Which Seemed to afford ample protection from the others

between 12 & 1 oclock We Received a veset from the Ietan Cheef the first time He Came near us Since We moved He Was very frendly and and Efected to know nothing of the difecuealty that had Existed—We Have Heare now about seven Hunderd lodges of the nations mentioned on the 25th With the addicion of the Cheans— about two Hunderd lodges—We Sopose those Lodges to Contain from twelve to twenty pursons of all Sises—Some Horses Have been Stollen Every night Since We arived amongst them Seven of our own are amongst the mising a party of one Hunderd and fifty men Went In pursute of the theefs but Returned Without overtakeing them— We Ware this day much afected by the arivel of Findley Who Head been absent from us 30 days alone and on foot He informed us that Ware parteys of Pannees Ware both behind and before Him tho He seen none—

28th nov 1821

about 10 oClock a party of 200 men Started the diferent nations to Reinforce a party gon before them In pursute of Stolen Horses

[110] [Evidently the Comanches, still angry at not having received "the goods . . . that His father the Presedent Had Sent them," and frustrated at not being able to take possession of Glenn's trading goods, had won over some of the Kiowas to their side. The old Kiowa chief who had remained with Glenn to forestall an attack went along with him to the new camp; but the threat was not yet at an end, even though the arrival of the friendly Arapahoes restored a balance of power favorable to the white men. With the arrival of the Cheyennes the lodges numbered nine hundred, and the Indians ten to eighteen thousand, following Fowler's estimates.]

With orders to Pursu till the Caught them—the Indeans manefest a more frendly disposion and Intimate an Intention of moveing down the River In Consequance of the many Horses Stolen from them Heare—between 4 and 500 Horses Have [been] Stolen from them Since We arived and mostly from the Pens in the Center of the vilege surrounded by upwards of seven Hunderd lodges of Wachfull Indeans—the Ware Parties Returned Without Efecting any thing Except those on foot Wore the Soles off their mockesons—

29th nov 1821

the Snow Has Intirely disappeered and the ground dry as dust— the Remainder of the War partey Have all Returned

on our Way up the River before our arivel at the Indeans Camp I broke one of the glasses out of my Specks—and on puting them on one day I soon felt the Hand of an Indean grasp them from my face He maid off as fast as poseble I gave up the Specks for lost but Head no moad of Replaceing them—In a Short time I Heard great Shouting and laffing and looking to See What Was the Caus I discovered the Indean that Head taken my Specks Leading an other With the Specks on His face the felow Was Led up to me and I was shoon that He Head but on Eye—and that the Specks Wold Sute Him better [than] me as the Head but one glass Heare Eanded the Joack the Returned the Specks in much good Humor amongst all the Ware present

30th november 1821

Pased this day With out any diffigualty Prepareing Some Hunters to trap in the mountains.

1st Decembr 1821

fine Weather nothing new—

2nd norr [Dec.] 1821

an alarm of the Enemy found two of the Horses Soposed to be stolen—the Ietan braught them In—the Hunters detained on act of an alarm—

3rd Decmbr 1821

Started the trappers under the Command of Slover—and With Him Simpson—maxwell—Pryer [111] Findley and Taylor

111 [Entries in the "Union Mission Journal" for December 10, 29, and 30, 1821, show that Captain Pryor was present at the mission on the Neosho River at this time. The evidence shows that the Pryor now with the Fowler expedition was a different man. "Union Mission Journal," *American Missionary Register*, II (May 1822), 431, 432.]

4th Decmbr 1821

Fine Weather for the Season this day termenated Without any difegualty—the Ietan Cheef Sick Sent for Conl glann to give Some medeson but declined In consequance of His former bad Conduct

6th Decm 1821

Fine Weather the Indeans talk of moveing the Buffelow are now drove to Some distance and this I [is] not to [be] thought Straing as about one Hunderd of them are Eaten In Camp Each day Sinc our aRivel

7th Decm 1821

Fine Weather—nothing new to day

8th Decm 1821

the morning fine Weather the Indeans Still talk of moving but as yet Remain Heare—the furnish [us] With Plenty of the best of buffelow meet at a low Rate bu do not Wish us to Hunt them our Selves— aledgeing We Wold drive the Buffelow all off the Ietan Cheef Calling fore Some medecon a day or two back and find[ing] His Complaint Was not dangerous Conl glann gave Him Some Rice and Black Pepper With derections to boil and make soop of it—to day He paid us a viset Pufed up and Well as Ever the Arrapoho Cheef Says He Was Restored to Health by the Same medeson—

9th Decmbr 1821

Fine Weather Continues—yesterday gave notice that Some Horses Wold be purchased but none Has maid their appeerence—

10th Decm 1821

yesterday purchased one very fine Hors from an Ietan at a High Price—the Weather fine this morning but the Wind from N W no more Horses offered this day—

11th

last night Was Clouday the River is now oppen Haveing thad [thawed] in the those last Warm days—the Weather is now Colder

12th Decm 1821

the Cold Weather Still Continues but the River is not frosen up yesterday a War partey Returned the Ware of the Ietans—With 28 Horses taken from the Crows on the River Platt below the mountains—the Ware five nights Returning the Ietans this day moved up the River We Ware unable to by any more Horses tho We offered High Prices

13th Decm 1821

last night the River frose up the Weather is very Cold the Indeans determen to move up the River for Wood and meet We offerd to go With them on the 15th Which Satisfyed them very much and they offered us Horses to Carry our goods but unable to make any more purchases for feer We leave them a the [as they] appeer much atached to us

14th Decmbr 1821

The Indeans Exspect to meet the Spanyerds[112] on the River above this place to traid With them this morning We Commenced packing up to move—

15th Decm 1821

the Indeans furnished us With Some Horses Which Inabled us to move With them up the River about five miles West[113] from our Camp and Heare Camped on the South Side of the River—but about one mile below Wheare We Camped the the Kiawa Cheef With His nation Had Stoped and Intended We Shold Stop With them but the Arropoho Cheef told us We Shold go to His Camp Which We

[112] [These Spaniards came from Taos or Santa Fe and apparently resembled the Comancheros from those places. The latter went along the Canadian River into the northern Llano Estacado to trade with the Comanches.

These parties of *Comancheros* are usually composed of the indigent and rude classes of the frontier villages, who collect together, several times a year, and launch upon the plains with a few trinkets and trumperies of all kinds, and perhaps a bag of bread and may-be another of *pinole*, which they barter away to the savages for horses and mules. The entire stock of an individual trader very seldom exceeds the value of twenty dollars. (Gregg, *Commerce of the Prairies*, p. 257)

They had come over the old Taos Trail, which ran from Santa Fe through Taos and the southeastern corner of the San Luis Valley, over Sangre de Cristo Pass, and along the Greenhorn and St. Charles rivers to the Arkansas at the site of Pueblo, Colorado. It was a shorter route from Santa Fe to the buffalo plains than the one running through San Miguel, across Raton Pass, and down the Purgatory River, which became the Santa Fe Trail.]

[113] To a position 2 or 3 m. beyond Nepesta, and about 5 m. short of Huerfano river.

[Pike camped on the evening of November 21, 1806, "about midway between Fowler and Napesta, Pueblo County, Colo. Napesta is little more than a highway marker." Jackson, *Journals of Zebulon Montgomery Pike*, I, 347 n.]

Intend to do but Heare a new diffqualty arises as the Clame us as
their frends—Which may lead to a Ware With them and destruction
to our Selves but this Was Soon got over as two of our men Stoped
with the Kiawa Cheef till He got in a good Hummor and telling Him
that He aught to go With us—that it Was Him that left us and not
We that left Him—With this He Was Satisfyed and one of the [men]
Remained With Him all night and frend Ship Was Restored the
Kiawas Came to our Camp as ushal—

16th Decm 1821
the man and load left With the Kiawas Was braught up and no
difequality than the Refuse to Sell us Horses Still feering We Will
leave them—but to day purchased 2 mules and three Horses from
the Arrapohos

17th Decm 1821
the Weather verry much moderated Haveing much the appeerence
of the Indean Sommer

more Sevelity Exsists amongst those Indeans than anny I have
Ever knone it is de[si]rable on that accoumpt not to Camp Seperate
from any of the Bands—but on the other Hand you are Continuly
Crouded With young men and old begers—We yet Want about ten
Horses—and all tho there is about 20 000 in our inCampment and
the [Indians are] distetute of Every thing—We are afraid We Will not
be able to obtain them the Arrapohoes Have but few in Com-
pareson With the others owing to their Haveing last Sommer
traided With Chians of the mesurey [Missouri]—the Ietan and Kiawa
Have great nombers of very fine Horses—and Equal to any I have
Ever knone—

18th Decm 1821
about ten oclock last night the Wind Chainged to the West and the
Weather Exstreemly Cold So that We Cold not do any thing—We
yesterday traided for two Horses and one mule—the Kiawas paid
us a viset and Invited us to a feest So We are frends again—

19th Decm 1821
the Cold In Creces So that it Is Imposeble to travel on the Pirarie
—the Children Have now fine Sport on the Ice

20 Decm 1821
at day light We Ware alarmed by the Sound of Heavey bloes Struck
by one Indean uppon an other Who Run towards our lodge and Was

persued with the tamehak at about one Rod distance a blo Was
Struck but the Indean Run Round our lodge—but Was overtaken
and Receved a Heavey blow on the Back of the neck Which felled
Him to the ground apperently dead—but but a nomber of Squas
Interfeered and Carryed off the Soposed dead Indean and Saved
His life—We find Him to be the Son of the Kiawa Cheef and first
frend amongst the Indeans His murdorer Was the brother of the
great Arrapoho Cheef and our frend and protecter We are now
feerful of the most Seerous Consequences as We are not able to Say
What may Happen betwen the two nations—as War betwen them
Wold be fatel for us

21st Decm 1821

the man Wounded yesterday is not dead and is likely to recover—the
Case of the atack on His Was the Steeling the medecen bagg of
the other Who Was a Cheef no other difequelty is apprehended as the
bagg is Returned and axepted—We have Sucseeded in purchasing as
many Horses as Will answer our Purposese of moveing—at night the
Snow began to fall—

22nd Decm 1821

the Ietan Cheef Has not viseted us Since He moved up the River in
Consequence of not Receveing Some presents He demanded on the
day He moved but the Braves appeer friendly this four days We
Calcolate on moveing on Crismus day to the mountains no Inter
Corse betwen the arrapoho and the Kiawa for two days

23rd Decm 1821

We Informed the Indeans that on the 25th We Wold move to the
mountains—at night Indeans Inform us of their detirmenation to
move With us—

24th Decm 1821

promising to move the arrapoho determened to acCompany us to
night Conl glann Sent for the Kiawa Cheef and paid for the use of
His lodge allso gave a meddle the likeness of genl Jacson Informed
Him it Was not the medle of His great father but it Was given Him
as a token of a great man and as the frend of the White men and
Charged Him at the Same time that When Ever He meet the White
man to treat Him frendly to Which He agread With great Satisfaction

25th Decm 1821

this morning the Conl gave the Ietan Cheef a shirt medle and Small presents With the Same Cerymones and promeses as the Kiawa yesterday last Evening We Sent for Him but being un Well and unable to Come He Sent His brother by Home [whom] We Sent [word] We Wold viset Him in the morning We found Him very un Well and discovered the the Indisposion Was the Caus of His not viseting us Since He moved up the River He Exspresed much frendship and Satisfaction—

the arrapoho move with us this morning.

It is but Justice to Say We find the Kiawa the best Indeans possing more firmness and manly deportment than the arrapoho and less arogance and Hatey Pride than the Ietan—we Ware In vited this day to Eat With one of the arrapoho Cheefs He Seet before us a dish of fat meat of Which We Eat plentyfully We Ware then asked if We new what kind of meat We Ware Eating We told We did not He then Said it Wa[s] a dog telling us it [was] a great feest With the Indeans— and that He Invited us for that purpose—

We move up the River West Eight miles and Camped on the South Side Crossing a fork[114] of the River at five miles this forke is Small and Heads to the South there is Some Cotten Wood a long its bottoms Which appeer to be very Rich and Wide Eknof for farms— the Arrapohos acompany us We Ware fortunate In parting With the Rest of our nibours With out any difequalty—We Have now in all thirty three Horses In Cludeing two belongeing to Peno one to Vanbeber two [to] J and R Fowler and two to Duglass one to Bono all in bad ordor—

26th Decm 1821

moved late In Consequence of lose[ing] Some of our Horses Which Ware not found till late In the day—our Corse South 70 West five miles[115]—We Camped on the South Side of the River to morrow the Indeans make a Hunt

[114] The Huerfano or Orphan river, falling into the Arkansaw as said, opposite the station Booneville on the railroad. See Pike, ed. of 1895, p. 448, for this river, which is his "2nd Fork." Among the mangled names found in print are Rio Walfano of Farnham, Travels, 1843, p. 41; and, most curious of all, Wharf creek of Long's Exped., ii, 1823, p. 59, where the innocent reader is informed that the Rio Huerfano "is called by the Spaniards Wharf creek, probably from the circumstance of its washing perpendicular precipices of moderate height"!

[115] From camp at a point given on the 25th as 3 m. above the Huerfano, to-day's 5 m. would take Fowler about 3 m. short of St. Charles river. He passes opposite the mouth of Chico creek, as duly noted on the 27th. See Pike, ed. of 1895, p. 451.

27th Decm 1821

We lay With the Indeans to let our Horses Eat Haveing kept them tyed up Sinc We Started yesterday Pased a [Chico] Crick on the north Side of the River its Corse is [from the] north—

28th Decembr 1821

We moved about 12 oclock and Went five miles up the River and Camped on the South Side Heare is the Statement of Conl glann on parting With the Arrapoho Cheef [116]

I never parted with a man who showed as much sorrow as the chief of the arrapoho He persuaded us very much to stay with him one moon longer—stating to us the danger of having our horses stolen &c &c but finding in the morning we determined to start he made no objection, after giving him a medal &c as I did to the other Chiefs— and making a small present with all of which he was much satisfied when I shook hands with him to start he threw himself on his bed in tears—after traveling about one mile we was overtaken by one of his brothers, a young chief with a request to incamp on this side as his brother was starting to follow so as to sleep one more night with us we are truly fortunate in having those 3 nations with us—

29th Decr

The chief did not arrive last night as he sent us word—but early

[116] At this point in the MS. the handwriting changes, Fowler's giving way to that of Colonel Glenn, who writes in a firm and clear hand. The reader will also notice the difference in the spelling and syntax of what now follows, to the middle of the account of Dec. 31.

[Glenn's decision to accompany the Spaniards to Taos was without doubt prompted by the information they gave him. On February 24, 1821, the independence of Mexico had been proclaimed in the Plan of Iguala. The revolutionary army led by Agustin de Iturbide entered Mexico City on September 27, while the Glenn-Fowler expedition was in eastern Oklahoma. News of the victorious entry reached Santa Fe on December 26, and the royal governor, Don Facundo Melgares, declared that January 6, 1822, should be a day of celebration. Glenn's informants would not have known the outcome of these events but they were clearly acquainted with some of the earlier developments. Meanwhile, William Becknell, who had left Arrow Rock, Missouri, on September 1, 1821, reached Santa Fe on November 16. There he sold his trading goods and started back toward the United States before the middle of December. Thomas James, who during August had talked with Glenn in Oklahoma about his proposed trip, arrived in Santa Fe about December 1. Hubert Howe Bancroft, *History of Arizona and New Mexico, 1530–1888* (San Francisco: History Company, 1889), pp. 308–9.]

next morning an express arrived to inform us that instant as he was starting Two spaniards[117] arrived and that a party of 60 were expected today with a request for us to return and see them—Mr Roy & myself immediatly returned, and rec^d with as much Joy and satisfaction by the village as if though we had been absent for one year the friendship which they shew us before the spaniards will convince them that sho^d the party expected be hostile we will have the friendship of the Indians and although my party is now only 13 men in all I fele no fear in meeting 60 Spaniards, with the multitude of the Indians

30th Decr

Yesterday at about 3 Oclock we went out to the Prarie to see if we could discover the spanish party—we discovered them about 5 miles distance, we advanced to meet them—when they discovered us they halted and formed to receive us in "military style"—we were requested by our Companion to Halt, when we were received on a full charge—To within ten paces of us when the men all dismounted and embraced us with affection and friendship—they are all creoles of that country—seem well disposed—possess far less sence than the Indeans we are with, seem happy and possess a greater degree of Joy at seeing us than could be Immagined—It is a matter of astonishment the difference of treatment of the Indians to them and our party—the Indians Commanded them as much as we command our negroes—At night the Indians asked us if we were willing to let the Capt. and his principle man sleep [in] the lodge with us, which we agreed to—the Indeans derected them to pray so that we may see their fashion which they readily agreed to and went through with the Catholic prayers, and afterwards prayed fervently for us—their whole trading equipment in the U. S. would not sell for fifty dollars—In short to describe them would require the pen of a Butler and the pencil of a Hogarth[118]—They leave here to morrow for home and I intend to accompany them—

31st Decr. It is only necessary to Judge of them to say the Capt. and all his party were painted like the Indians the day they traded—and during the prayer the Capt. Caught a louse on his shirt and eat it—[119]

[117] [These were the Spaniards mentioned in the entry for December 14.]

[118] [Glenn was evidently referring to one of several editions of Samuel Butler's *Hudibras*, with illustrations by William Hogarth.]

[119] At this point Fowler resumes his own pen, but Colonel Glenn's story continues, apparently by dictation to Fowler, to the end of the entry for Jan. 1, 1822.

the Spaniards moved up to our Camp from the Indeans for the purpose of [selling] us Some Corn the no [they know] nothing about our moad of measurement but ask at the Rate of ten dollers pr Bushil the ask thirty dollers for a mule and one Hunderd dollers for ther best Running Horses—We Intend leaveing this With the Spanierds in the morning—

January 1st 1822

this being a holaday With our nibours[120] We lay by all day— Haveing about two pounds of bacon Which I Head kept as a Reserve I Heare Shewd it to the Indeans—the Cheef asked What kind of anemel maid that meat When He Was told a Hog He Requested the Shape of it to be maid on the Sand When that Was [done] all the Indeans said the Head never Seen Such an animal and appeered to Wonder and think it Strange that the Head never Seen the like Soposing them Selves to Have Seen all kind of anemels—

I Heare left mager Fowler in Charge of the Camp[121] With Instructions to fortify His Camp and Hors Peen to treat all Indeans frendly but traid With none—and shold War party Call to let them Have Some Powder ball and Paint With Some tobaco

on the 30th ultimo three of our [men] Ware Sent out to the mountains to Hunt for Buffelow and Ware meet by a party of thirteen Indeans of the Crowes Haveing With them about two Hunderd Horses Which the Had Stolen from Some other nation and Ware on theer Way Home—the took our men Prisnors as fare as the River Wheare the took from them their Powder ball and Blankets giveing them nine fine Horses in payment for What the Head taken While this traid Was progresing the Horses Ware Crossing on the Ice—a Ware Party of arrapohoes over took them a battle Was the Consequence and Each party took off part of the Horses and our men maid their Escape In the Battle leaveing all the Horses the Head obtained of the Indeans—the Ware treated frendly by the Crowes and tolled the Ware taken only to prevent them from giveing Information to the arrapohoes—the Crowes Say the left the White People on the Platt[122] about 10 nights ago and that it Will

---

[120] [The Spaniards.]

[121] [The entry for January 1, 1822, and the license granted by Major William Bradford leave no doubt that Glenn was the leader of the expedition and Major Fowler was second in command.]

[122] [This party of thirty-five has not been identified. Perhaps the men were French traders or trappers.]

take them three nights to go there With their Horses Wheare the left
the Rest of their nation—the speeke on the most frendly terms of the
White men and Say the are about 35 in nomber—all the nesecery
araingements are maid for my Self and four men to Set out in the
morning to Cross the mountains to Santafee—[123]

Jany 2nd 1822

this morning the Spanierds Began to Collect their Horses and load
for their departure—Conl glann and four men Set out With them—
leaveing me With Eight men in an oppen Camp With the ballence of
the goods after takeing Some things With Him to Sell So as to pay
their Exspences. We are now In the Hart of the Inden Cuntry and
Emedetly on the great Ware Road—not only of one nation against
the others—in the Road to all the Spanish Settlements With Which
the Indeans on this Side of the mountains are at War—So that our
Setuation is not of the most Plesent kind—We Have no meet In
Camp—and Con Clude to Send two Hunters out With Horses in the
morning to kill Some meat Intending to Set the ballence of the Hands
at Work to build a Hous and a Strong Peen for the Horses at night

Jany the 3rd 1822

Roas Early to Start the Hunters ordered two of the men[124] to Prepare

[123] Santa Fé, N. M.—End of Colonel Glenn's story, in Fowler's handwriting.
[At this time the entire expedition may be counted. Lewis Dawson was dead.
Slover, Simpson, Maxwell, Pryor, Findlay, and Taylor, who all had been sent into
the mountains on December 3, returned about noon on January 11. Remaining
with Major Fowler were his brother Robert, his servant Paul, and six other men,
who are mentioned by name in subsequent entries: George Douglas, Eli Ward,
Jesse Van Bibber, Dick Walters, and the two French hunters Jacques Bono and
Joseph Barbo. Three of the four men who accompanied Glenn to Taos were
Baptiste Moran, Baptiste Peno, and Baptiste Roy. The fourth man accompanying
Glenn must have been the twenty-first member of the expedition. See note 12
above.]

[124] [The two men who lay still and the five who "Seperated to them Selves" a
little later in the morning are not named, but their identity may be guessed.
Robert Fowler sided with his brother. Jacob Fowler felt himself secure with Paul
(January 10 and 27) and subsequently appeared on cordial terms with him (February 10), and Paul was probably on his side. Fowler showed a sympathetic
interest in Dick Walters (February 4) and later (February 12) chose him to be the
fourth member of his trapping party, with Robert Fowler and Paul. (Taylor,
the fifth member of Fowler's trapping party was in the mountains with Slover at
the time of this confrontation). On the other hand Fowler soon showed some
mistrust of Eli Ward and was not altogether sympathetic toward him during the
incident of the Indian horse and the mule (January 4). Ward and George Douglas

the Horses While the Hunters got Readey—but the men lay Still I
maid the Second Call but With no better Sucsees—I then discovered
that a mutney Was Intended—and Emedetly drew one of the men
from His beed by the top of His Head. but [one] of his frends in the
Plott asisted Him—and We Ware Soon all In a Scoffel. but Robert
Fowler Soon Came to my asistance—and the bisness as Soon
Ended—tho it Was Some time before the gave up their Intended
muteney and five of them Seperated to them Selves and declared the
Wold do the plased and Wold not be ordered by any other porson—
I soon discovered that the Exspected the Spanierds Wold not let
Conl glann Return and that they Intended to make the best of the
goods the Cold—aledgeing the Ware the Strongest party and that
the Wold pay them Selves—on Which discovery I told them that un
less the Wold Return to their dutey I Wold send for the Arrapoho
Cheef Who Wold be gld to asist me to take Care of the goods and that
the might go Whare the plased—and that I Wold not Suffer them to
meddle With the goods—the then Held a Councle and sent one man
to tell me that If I Wold be acountable to them for their pay—the
Wold go to their dutey and do What I ordored them—to Which I
toled them I wold make no new Bargen With them—and that If the
Chose the might go on With their mutenous Sceen—that I Cold
protect the goods till the Indeans Came for Which I Wold Soon
Send—the then all Came and Stated that the Wold do What I told
them and Wold go to Work Emedetley—and asked me to think of
them and Secure the pay for them If Conl glann Shold not Return
Which the Espected He never Wold. and that it Wold be Heard for
them to loos all their Wages—to Which I toled them if the Continued
to do as good and Honest men aught that as fare as the goods Wold
Reech they Shold be paid—the two men Went out to Hunt but
Returned With out killing any thing—now all Hands Went to
Worke Willingly and by night We Head the Hors Peen finished and
the Hous With two pens four logs High—Which maid part of the
Hors Pen and the door of the Hous in the Hors Peen Which Was So

---

appear to have been compatible (March 8 and 9) and may have joined the expedition together. The two French hunters were not associated with each other
in Fowler's account (Barbo was sometimes with Peno or Simpson), but they
probably had a common language and experiences, and perhaps common
interests and attitudes. The "five" may have been Douglas, Ward, Bono, Barbo,
and Van Bibber. The decisive act in quelling the resistance was probably Fowler's
threat to send for the Arapaho chief.]

Strong that a few Indeans Cold not take the Horses out With out Choping Some of the logs—and must Waken us all tho We Slept Ever So Sound—

Friday 4th Jany 1822

Went to Work Early got our House nine loggs High—and began to pitch the tents on the top by Way of a Roof the House Just Wide Enof for that purpose We Heared a gun near Camp two of the Hunters out We Soon Heared another and then Several others I took up my gun and Went to the plase Whear Robert Fowler Head killed two deer and Wounded Several more Heare We met With Ward With one deer and one turkey We Have now plenty of meet the first We Have Head for five days all Which time We lived on Corn precured from the Spanierds—

yesterday While we Ware building our House the Arrapoho Cheef and two of His Brothers Came to our Camp With one mule We had lost While With them—for Which I gave them Some presents—one of them Went to our Horses and Caught Hold [of] one Which Ward Head braught in a few days ago Which He Soposed the Crows Had lost—but the Arrapoho Clames—and I have no doupt of His being the oner—Ward derectly asked the Indean for presents Stating that I Head given them Some thing for finding the mule that He Wanted Some for finding the Horse—but this demand ofended the Indeans He Stated that the did not Cut off the mules tail to alter its looks as Ward Had don the Hors—and throing down What the Head Receved said the Wold keep the mule and that they Head lost three Horses and Soposed that Ward Head taken them all and that the other two Ware yet among our Horses and Went and looked—but Cold find no more—I told them there Was but one braught to Camp and that Ward Had don Rong to Cut the Horses tail—that He Head allso don Wrong to ask any thing I gave them up the Hors and told them to take What I Head given them—Presented the pipe Which the Smoked beged Some Powder and Bullets Which gave them—the are now quite pleased—Set off to go to their Camp Huging us all before the Start telling us the move Camp to morrow and Will meet us in the Spring on the River as We go down

Saterday 5th Jany 1822

three men Went With Horses on the Hunt of Buffelow but Re-turned With out seeing any this day finished our House and Packed in all the goods

Sunday 6th Jany 1822
Went up to the Warm Spring Branch [125] and Soot two traps but the
Weather is So Cold I beleve the bever Will not Come out—duglass

[125] Fontaine qui Bouille of the French, Boiling Spring river or creek, present
Fountain river or creek, site of the city of Pueblo. This river is Fontaine-qui-
bouit in Frémont, Fontequebouir in Farnham, Rio Almagre of the Spanish, and
forms one of the Grand Forks of Pike. See Pike, ed. 1895, p. 452, etc.
We must pause to consider Fowler as the first settler, or at least squatter, on
the site of the future Pueblo, Col., the honor of founding which is claimed by,
and commonly conceded to, James P. Beckwourth, whose mendacity was as
illimitable as the plains over which he roamed while he was the great chief of the
Crows, and whose credit for the same was as high as the mountains in which his
adopted nation lurked. It is true that Pike built at Pueblo a sort of stockade for
the defense of his party, but this was merely a log pen or breastwork which his
men occupied Nov. 24–29, 1806, while he went on a side trip to his peak. The
structure was such as could be thrown up over night, and all trace of it speedily
disappeared. But Fowler built a habitable house and horse-corral, which he
occupied about a month, while his party were trapping, hunting, and herding
their stock in the vicinity, awaiting the appointed time to take up the Taos Trail
which Col. Glenn had already followed to Santa Fé. The site of Pueblo does not
appear to have been reoccupied in any way that can be called settling, for 20
years after Fowler. Then the redoubtable Jim appears upon the scene: see
Leland's ed. of Bonner's Life of Beckwourth, 1892, p. 383. "We reached the
Arkansaw about the first of October, 1842, where I erected a trading-post, and
opened a successful business. In a very short time I was joined by from fifteen to
twenty free trappers, with their families. We all united our labors, and constructed
an adobe fort sixty yards square. By the following spring we had grown into quite
a little settlement, and we gave it the name of Pueblo." In so saying, this bound-
less liar tells the truth—whether by accident or design is immaterial to the sub-
stantial accuracy of what he says. We also read further in Inman, p. 252: "The
old Pueblo fort, as nearly as can be determined now, was built as early as 1840,
or not later than 1842, and, as one authority asserts, by George Simpson and his
associates, Barclay and Doyle. Beckwourth claims to have been the original
projector of the fort, and to have given the general plan and its name, in which
I am inclined to believe he is correct; perhaps Barclay, Doyle, and Simpson were
connected with him, as he states that there were other trappers, though he mentions no names. It was a square fort of adobe, with circular bastions at the
corners, no part of the walls being more than eight feet high. Around the inside
of the plaza, or corral, were half a dozen small rooms inhabited by as many
Indian traders and mountain-men." According to Fitzpatrick, in 1847 the settlement contained about 150 men and 60 or more women, the former mostly
Missourians, French-Canadians, and Mexicans, whose wives were squaws of
various Indian tribes, together with some American Mormon women. On this
subject see also Pike, ed. of 1895, pp. 453, 454, where an adobe fort is noted.
[See also Hart and Hulbert, *Zebulon Pike's Arkansaw Journal*, pp. 124–25.]

in the Evening on driveing up the Horses Reports Some Buffelow In
Sight the Hunters Will look for them In the morning

monday 7th Jany 1822

Went out to look for the Buffelow Seen them but killed none—
Went With Robert Fowler to the traps—Caught nothing on our
Return We Went to the Washed Rock as We Called it Which
Stands near the Bace of the Second bottom or low Hills the are about
fifty feet Higher than the low Bottom and Exstend back to Some
miles With out Riseing much Higher it appeers that this High land
Exstended once Round this Rock and has been Washed a Way by
the River the Rock is about ten feet Higher than the Highest land
in the nibour Hood and in the neck of low ground betwen a point
of from 5 to 7 acers nearly Squair—and the High lands back of the
bottom—and In my openion the best Setuation In all this Section of
the Cuntry for a garison as it is near Wood and Watter Which is in
the River about 100 yds on the South West side of this table and
about 50 yds from the above Rock Which [is] only asendable on the
East Side Round on the top about fifteen feet diameter—a stone
Wall is Raised on the margin of Such a Hight that a man may Sett
With Safty from Small army in the nibor Hood and about twelve
men might [illegible] With Convenence this Rock is about 400
Hunderd yds from the mouth of the Warm Spring branch Which is
West from th Rock and Heads to the north its bottoms a bout ½ a
mile Wide—a large River bottom on the South and West mostly
Pirarie—the High Ridge Exstends from the Rock about South
East—this Crick Contains Watter soffecent for mills and With a
long Raice plenty of fall may be Head—

tusday 8th Jany 1822

Went up to the mouth of the Crick from that to the Hill mentioned
yesterday and looking up the River Seen the glisning of a gun barrel
or Swoard blaid but Cold See nothin Elce Returned to Camp

Wensday 9th Jany 1822

my Self Robert Fowler and Jesey Vanbeber Went on Hors back to
look for Buffelow on the South Side of the River at about one and a
Half miles up the River We Ware Stoped by Vanbeber Calling to us
that He Seen Seven or Eight Indeans on the Pirarie on the north Side
of the River—that He Seen their gunbarrels gleson tho at about

three miles distance We Returned to Camp Emedetly—and Head the Horses drove up and garded the ballence of the day—tho We Seen nothing more of the Indeans—I Exspect the Ware a War party looking for the Arrapoho to Steel their Horses and that the Head Seen nothing of us or the Wold Have paid us a viset—

thorsday 10th Jany 1822

Went out on the South Side of the River took Pall With me I went about three miles over leavel Loos Sandey land to a High Ridge from Which We Seen one Buffelow about 2 miles beyound us—We Returned to Camp Killed nothing—the Hunters killed nothing—our meet scarce this morning Head the Ice Sanded So as to make a Road for the Horses fine grass on the north Side We put them over and Return them at night in to the Pen Whear We feed them With the tops of the Young Cotten Wood—of Which the are very fond

Friday 11th Jany 1822

Sent the Horses over Early. duglas to Hord them as Has been the Case Ever Since the Conl left us. one man all day With the Horses and drive them up at night the Wach by day is taken by turns amongest the Hands We Have now thirty Horses In Cluding those belonging to Indeviduels—about 12 oclock the Hunters Came In from the mountains Six in nomber the Weather Is So Cold the Cannot trap the Have Caught only Seven Bever killed Some deer Ealk and buffelow our Hunters kill one deer this day our Sperets are a little Raised We are now fifteen [126] In nomber and this party bringing in With them Six Horses and two mules We have thirty Eight [127] In all

Saterday 12th Jany 1822

Sent four Hunters With Seven Horses on the South Side of the River to the mountains to Hunt Buffelow and not to Return In less than three days Sent the Horses over the River to Paster—With Barbo to Hord them Who braught them all In at night

Sunday 13th Jany 1822

Sent the Horses over the River Dick Walters to Hord them—all Returned Safte at night—the Hunters not Returned—

[126] [The explicit numbering confirms the evidence of January 1. See note 123 above.]

[127] [In spite of the reluctance of the Indians to part with their horses, the traders now have eight more than they had when they started.]

monday 14th Jany 1822

Sent the Horses over the River With Bono to atend them—He killed one Deer and Braught it to Camp the Hunters Returned With Small Buffelow—the Head Killed Several old ones but the Ware Poor and left out the Horses all up at night

tusday 15th Jany 1822

drove the Horses over the River on the Ice as ushal—I then Went to look out a good Setuation for a new Settlement on the north Side of the River—Intending to move tomorrow Should no acoumpt Reach us from Conl glann—as We began to Sopose He Is now not at liverty to send or Return there being the full time Elapsed in Which He promised to Send an Exspress—and We think that a party of Spanirds may be Sent to take us prisnors—for Which Reason Intend makeing a Strong Hous and Hors Pen on the Bank of the River Wheare it Will not be In the Powe of an Enemy to aproch us from the River Side—and Shold the Spanierds appeer In a Hostill manner We Will fight them on the Ameraken ground. the River Hear being the line by the last tretey—the Horses all up at night

Wensday 16th Jany 1822

moved Camp Early up the River on the north Side to the Spot I looked out yesterday—We Built a Strong Hors Peen and Put up the Horses at night—no Word from Conl glann—We begin to Conclude as Is not Well Him [all is not well with him]

thorsday 17th Jany 1822

Sent the Horses out to grase With Dick Walters to atend them Robert Fowler and my Self Each Shott one aughter [otter] on the Ice the Horses all up at night no Word from Conl glann We Intend building a Hous to morrow about one Hour In the night thirty Indeans of the Crows Came In to our Camp and Ware frendly Recogniseing the three men the maid Prisnors on the 30th of last month and Exspressed much Joy to See them. and that the Head got Saft out of the fight With the Arrapohos—Stateing the Ware going to War With that nation We gave them Plenty of boiled meet of Which the Eat Hartily I gave them Some tobaco to Smoke—after the Head don Eating and Smokeing the Sung a long Song and all lay down and Slept tell morning—

Friday 18th Jany 1822

the Cheef this morning asked for Some tobaco Powder and lead for His People Which I gave Him With Which he appered Well Pleesed and gave me a Hors and I then [gave him] four knives—the Indeans begun now to move off—but takeing What the Cold lay their Hands on—one of our men lost a Pistle I toled [the] Cheef Who Returned [it] Emedetly—and Caused all to be Returned He Cold but Some of the Indeans Head gon before the artickels Ware mised on fellow Came In to my tent threw down His old Roab and took a new one— I took it from Him and toled Him to take His own—and on His takeing it took my Saddle bagg all So—I took them from Him and Pushed Him out of the tent—by this time one of the [men] Called out the an Indean Was going off With His Blanket I applyed to the Cheef Who followed the fellow and braught back the blanket—but the fellow Coming back Presented His gun at Simpson—on Which We Ware all Redey for Battle In an Instent but the Indean let down His gun Picked up an old Roab He Had left as it appeered in place of the blanket the Cheef then moved them all off before Him—but after the Ware gon Several things Ware missing amongst the Rest a Roal of large Brass Wier three blankets five knives a smelting ladle and Dick Walters Shot pouch and Powder Horn With their Contents the Cheef toled me the Ware In Sarch of the Arrapohos Who He Said Head left [this] part of the Cuntry [128] and gon to the South that He Wold Return Home to the River Wheare the White men Ware traid Ing With His nation and Stated that the Whites Ware Sixty five in nomber—the Indeans Have Eaten up nearly all our meet and We feel alarmed least the Shold Return—and Soon Set about building a Hous—nor did We let out the Horses till We Ware Well ashored the Indeans Ware all gone off—

We built the Hous With three Rooms and but one out Side door and that Close to the Hors Pen So that the Horses Cold not be taken out at night Without our knoledge We got the Hous Seven logs High and Well Chinked the goods al stoed a Way before night—two of our Hunters Went Some distance on the Indean trail and See two of them Sitting on a Hill as a Rear gard—and on our men Returning the Cold See three Indeans following them Some distance but least the Should Come back and take our Horses the Ware all drove Into

[128] [Presumably the departure of the Arapahoes meant that the trading for which the Indians had assembled on the upper Arkansas was now over.]

the Peen and garded the balence of the day and all night—We now felled trees a Cross the Hors Peen So that it Was Imposeble for the Indeans to take the Horses out With out Choping them off and our door and Hors Peen door Ware So Setuated that [they] Cold not be taken out With out our knoledge as We kept two Sentnals all night and all the men Slept With their armes Readey beleveing the Indeans from the disposetion Shoon to Steell When the left us Wold Return at night and Steel our Horses—

Satterday 19th Jany 1822
Sent out the Horses Early and Bono to Watch them—the Ware all up at night and two Sentnals up all night We See nothing of the Indeans but Exspect them In a few days—the Cheef toled us He Exspected to Return In a few days and that We Shold move up betwen the mountains out of the Ware path [129] that a great many parteys Wold Com this Way and Wold Steel all our Horses and take our goods to avoid Which We must go up betwen the mountains out of their Way and Whear there Was plenty of deer Elk and Buffelow and that as the White mans frend He Wold viset us there—

How Ever good this advice I Cold not Pursue it till the time Sott by Conl glann to Return Shold Run out Which Wold be on the 2nd day of febury—and if He did not come by that it Wold be becaus He [was] detained a prisnor—and then I was to go Whear I thaught best

Sunday 20th Jany 1822
the Horses out Early Ward and maxwell to gard them—Robert Fowler and Slover Caught one bever and a bever took off our trap Which appeers Was Swept a Way by the Runing of the Ice—I sott 2 traps In the Evening the Horses all up at night

Monday 21st January 1822—
I Caught one large bever this morning—and Slover a Small one—the Horses out Early—We are all most out of meet—and our Corn begining to be Scarce Con Clude to Send Hunters out tomorrow to kill buffelow Horses all up at night

tusday 22nd Jany 1822
I Sent off three men with four Horses to kill Buffelow Findley out to Wach the Horses Caught one Bever the Hunters Return at night but

[129] [The chief's advice was good, for the traders were camped squarely on the old Spanish-Indian trail that was taken by war and raiding parties from the north into New Mexico.]

killed nothing found one found one mair Soposed to Have been Stolen by the Indeans found two Horses and braught them to Camp— Seen one other Hors the did not take Will go after Him to morrow Horses all up at night

Wensday 23rd Jany 1822

Horses out Early—High Wind and Clear—tho a little Cloudey before day light—the Hole of this month up to this time Clear Hard frosts at night the last ten days Warm the Ice Which Was Eighteen [inches] thick on the River is nearly gon and the River oppen—Caught one bever and lost one trap Which Caught a bever Which pulled up the Stake to which the trap Was fasned and all Went off together—the Horses all up at night two of the men drove a Hors Soposed to Have Strayed from the Indeans—the men now begin to gro verey un Easey no Word from the Conl—He promised to Send Peno back in fifteen days it is now twenty three days and no Word We Exspect they are all prisnors—and that a party of Spanierds to take [us] will be Heare Shortly but them We Intend to fight and not be taken and not leeve our House till the month is out—and then go to Some Secure place in the mountains and Remain traping and Hunting till the grass groes So that our Horses Can travel a Cross the grand Pirarie and then make our Way Home

thorsday 24th Jany 1822

the Horses Sent out Early Simpson to atend them—Slover and Robert Fowler Caught one bever—the men maid Soap yesterday and this day the are Washing their Cloths four men out to try and kill Some der—Findley Caught one bever I am feerfull of sending to any great distance from Camp least the Spanierds Shold make an atack on us in their absence—and We not Strong Enf to keep them off—In the Evening I found one of the lost traps With a large bever In it the Horses all up at night no Word from the Conl—

Friday 25th Jany 1822

the Horses out as ushal—Ward [and] Bono killed a buffelow bull Braught In Some of the meat it Was not fatt—taylor Road out to Hunt this morning Has not Returned—the Horses all up at night—

Saterday 26th Jany 1822

Horses out as ushal—this morning a little Cloudy and looks like Rain of Which We Have Seen not more than Wold Wet a mans

Shirt Since We left White River in October last taylor Returned—
but killed nothing—the Horses all up at night two Bever Ware
Caught this day—

Sunday 27th Jany 1822

the Horses Sent out Early I too[k] Pall With me and Road up the
north fork on the Warm Spring branch about three miles no Ice to
be Seen Except a little on the Shores from Hear I Crossed the Cuntry
to the main River a distance of a bout five miles and Struct the River
a bout three miles above the forkes Heare the River Has all the
appeerence of a Clos Hard Winter the Ice is Close and Strong all
over the River down to the forks While below as far as We Have been
for a few days the there Is but little Ice to be Seen and a long the
Shores—the Watter from the Warm Spring must Shorly be the
Caus—five Bever Braught Into Camp this day the Horses all up at
night—

monday 28th Jany 1822

the Horses out as ushal and about ten oclock two of the men Came
Running In to Camp and Stated the Indeans Ware Cetching all the
Horses—Which to us Was very unwelken nuse as part of the men
Ware out So that We Cold not Spair men anof to fight them on the
Pirarie—but In a few minets the Horses took the alarm and broak
from the Indeans and Came Runing to Camp—and Was followed by
the Indeans. but Heare the Horses did not stop but took to the Pirarie
and the Indeans gave up the Chais—and Came to us as frends—the
Ware the Same party of Crows that Ware With us a few days back
and that Head Stolen So many things from us When the Ware going
a Way I Emedetly Sent Some men after the Horses and Head them
Shet up In the Pen—In the main time treeted the Indeans frendly
give them Some tobaco to smoke and boiled meat to Eat but Put
all the men to Wach as We new them to be theves It appeer the Have
been In pursute of the Arrapoho but Have not bee able to tak
Horses as the are all Returning on foot—and Will take our Horses if
the Can their Hole party is now Collected and the are twenty Seven
In nomber that [is] three less than When the left us—the Say the Had
a fight With the Arrapoho and killed five and I Sopose the lost the
three mising—but now our men are all Collected and the Horses
fasned up in the Peen We think our Selves a full match for this party
—the then offered me Some Roaps in Exchaing for tobaco Which I

gave them as We Wanted Some Roaps the Chief then asken me for
Some Powder Balls Paint and virdegrees—I gave Him a ltle of
Each think Ing that if I gave Him What He asken for the Wold not
Steel—but in that I was mistaken for When the begun to move of the
began to Steel but two kittles being mised the Cheef maid Serch and
found [one] the other He Cold not find—and Said the fellow that
took it Had gon off—the now appeer to be all Readey to Start—and
about ten of the go to the Hors Peen and Exmen it and I beleve the
Intend takeing all the Horses—I ordeared all the men to Stand
Readey With His [gun] In His Hand but not to use it till I Shot
first—my Intention Was to avoid a fight If poseble—but not to let
them take our Horses—but after looking Some time Round the
Peen—the Cheef Spoke and Said you aught not to Stay Heare the
Indeans Will take your Horses—go to mountains out of this Ware
Road—I am the White mans frend and do not Want the Indeans
to take your Horses—He then Shook Hands to go off—and one of
His Cheefs Stole a bridle and put it in His bosem—Which I seen I
Pulled oppen His Roab and took the Bridle from Him the then
moved off about fifty yds and all stoped and appeered to prepair for
Battle With their Backs towards us—We Ware Ready for battle but
intend[ed] to let them brake the peece first but the Cheef looking
Round to us and Pointing to the Pirarie Called out tabebo [130]
Which We understood to be White men—and Heare a new difecuelty
presents its self—these Indeans are at War With the Spanierds and
if that Shold be Conl glann With His party the Indeans Will Sopose
them Spanierds and atack them—but to Prevent that two of our
men Run threw the Indeans and Joined the men [131] and Came With

[130] Compare "'tabba bone!' which in the Shoshonee language means white
man," Lewis and Clark, ed. of 1893, p. 480.

[131] [Again they were providentially saved from disaster, for the Indians very
likely meant to take Fowler's horses. Glenn had gone to Taos and then to Santa
Fe, where probably he arrived during the week of January 13. He returned to
Taos before the end of the week and shortly afterward employed a number of
men (including one "Battees") to accompany Baptiste Peno on his return to
Fowler's camp on the Arkansas River. The frequency with which the name Peno
(or Pino, as it is spelled in Glenn's license) appears in New Mexican records opens
the possibility that this man may have come originally from New Mexico.

M. M. Marmaduke, traveling southwest, stayed on July 22, 1824, at the
"ranche" of Juan Peno, three days' travel from San Miguel. "This man is
wealthy," he wrote, "having 160,000 head of sheep, and many cattle, horses and
mules" ("M. M. Marmaduke Journal," in Hulbert, *Southwest on the Turquoise*

them up to Camp and the Indeans Receved them as frends it proved
to be Peno and Some Spanierds Sent by Conl glann to Conduct us
to the Spanish Settle ment Wheare the govenor and People Head
Recd Him on the most frendly terms and thus our feer from that
quarter Ware all Removed along With Peno there Was a french
Indean or Half Breed that Spoke the Cro language We now Held
a Counsel as our talk Heare to fore Was mostly by Signs. Heare our
terms of frendship Was Renued the Cheef Stateing that He Hated
that His nation Shold be Called theves that He Wold as much as
poseble Hender them from Steeling that He Had Cursed them for
Steeling but Cold not find the Kittle—Still telling us to go to the
mountains and out of the War Path that He Had Hard Work to
keep His People from Steeling our Horses—at the Eand of the talk
I gave them Some Powder and tobaco—the Shok Hand and moved
off—the Weather Became Cloudey and about dark Began to Snow a
little

tusday 29th Jany 1822

Sent the Horses out Early the Hands to Packing up the goods So as
to Set out in the morning for the Spanish Settlement[132] agreable to
advice from Conl glann We now under Stand that the mackeson
[Mexican] provence Has de Clared Independance of the mother
Cuntry and is desirous of a traid With the people of the united
States Conl glann also advises me that He Has obtained premition
to Hunt to trap and traid In the Spanish provences—

Wensday 30th Jany 1822

We moved about ten oclock and Steered a little South of the 3rd
mountain over a level plain[133] about ten miles to a Crick a bout 30
feet Wide and Runs north East and Heads in the mountains the
Bottoms in this Crick is from three to four Hunderd yards Wide and
Well Covered With Cotten Wood and Boxelder the Bluffs about one

---

Trail, p. 74). Becknell at "St. Michael" (San Miguel) on November 14, 1821,
said, "Fortunately I here met with a Frenchman, whose language I perfectly
understood, and hired him to proceed with us to Santa Fe, in the capacity of
interpreter." William Becknell, "Journal of Two Expeditions from Boone's Lick
to Santa Fé," p. 63.]

132 [Taos.]

133 [The route they are now following was that old Spanish-Indian trail
between Taos and the Arkansas River which Paul and Pierre Mallet had followed
in 1739–40.]

Hunderd feet High frunted With [stone] of a grayis Coller and to appeerence Weell adapted for Building—the Hunters killed two Buffelow Bulls—

S° 25 West 10 miles [134]

Wensday [Thursday] 31st Jany 1822

Set out about 10 oclock and at about two miles [s]truck the Spanish Road on our left Hand—which leads to touse [Taos, N.M.] Which We followed and at five miles fell on a branch of the Crick on Which We lay last night—the meet about one mile below our Camp—We kept up this Crick and out at the Head of it and over a low Ridge to another Branch of the Same Crick Which Puts in below the forkes of the other—We Went up this Crick about one mile and Camped near the Mountain makeing about 10 miles in all and a little West of South—the Hunters killed three deer and four Buffelow one of Which Was two Poor for use and two left out all night the Hunters being alone and not able to bring in the meet and it Was lost—deer is plenty Heare but Wild We Will Stay Heare to morrow for the Purpose of killing meet to load the Spare Horses—

S° 25 West 10 miles [135]

thorsday [Friday] 1st Feby 1822

Hunters out Early—killed one Cow Buffelow With In four Hunderd yards of Camp—but So Poor the meat Was not Worth Saveing— three Bulls killed this day and three Hors loads of meat Braught to Camp—two deer braught into Camp—it is now Sunddown and three Hunters out yet—this morning Was Clouday and the Snow fell about 2 Inches deep—about 10 oclock at night the Hunters Came In Haveing killed three Buffelow and loaded their Horses to Camp one of them Slover—got His feet a lletle frost Bitten—Conclude to Hunt to morrow as our Horses Can Carry more meet

[134] From Pueblo, Col., to a point on the Rio San Carlos or St. Charles river, the creek above said, which is struck a little above the confluence of the Greenhorn branch. See Pike, ed. of 1895, p. 451. The San Carlos is Pike's "3d Fork" of the Arkansaw.

[135] Approximately up the Greenhorn to a point near lat. 38° N. The sources of the Greenhorn are several, flowing from the mountain of the same name (Spanish Cuerno Verde), 12,230 or 12,341 feet high, near the southern end of the Wet Mountain range.

At this date Fowler duplicates the day of the week, which throws him out till Feb. 9, when he corrects himself. But there is no break in days of the month.

Friday [Saturday] 2nd Feby 1822

up Early to Start the Hunters out—but I now discover the men are all feerfull of meeting With the Indeans as We are near the War Road and Have maid So much Sign In the Snow that the Will track us up and Steel our Horses Whill We are So much Scattered as not to be able to defend our Selves—and to be left Heare Without Horses—at So great a distance from Home—there is no knolede of What destress We might Come to—

I then Con Cluded to load up and move on the Road Which We did and on loading up the Horses We find seven Hors loads of meet We moved on about six miles along the futt of the mountains to [a] Crick [136] Wheare We Camped for Wood and Watter—the Hunters killed two Bulls this day but two Poor for use—the Snow is Heare about three Inches deep on the leavel Pirarie but on the north Side of the Hills the old Snow is more than one futt deep and up the mountains it is Still deeper—

S° 25 West 6 miles

Satterday [Sunday] 3rd Feby 1822

Set out Early about South along the foot of the mountains for about ten miles to a Crick [137] [and] about five miles [further] to Whar there the Remains of a Spanish fort to apperence ocepied about one year back—Hear We Camped [138] for the night Which Was

[136] One of the sources of the Greenhorn.

[137] Apache creek, a branch of Rio Huerfano, arising with sources of the Greenhorn from the mountain of the latter name, and flowing eastward.

[138] Fowler's distances seem to me short, considering how soon he is to make the Sangre de Cristo Pass for which he is heading, and I cannot locate this camp exactly. But his approximate position is easily made out. He is about to round the southern end of the Wet Mountain range, marked by Badito Cone, where the Rio Huerfano flows out to the plains; he will cross this river and enter upon the Sangre de Cristo range between the Sheep mts. and the Veta mts. His position is not far from lat. 37° 45'; place called St. Mary's in the vicinity. Fowler has come all along at an increasing distance W. of the D. and R.G.R.R., his route being the old "Taos Trail" which the Mexicans followed in passing from the Rio Grande in the vicinity of Taos to the Arkansaw at or near present Pueblo, Col.

[The Spanish fort had been built in 1819 by Governor Melgares to defend the pass against the encroachment by Americans. It was the northernmost Spanish outpost beyond Taos and is said to have been the only Spanish fort built in Colorado. Vestiges of the fort were identified and explored in the 1920s by Claud Swift of Walsenburg, Colorado, former sheriff of Huerfano County. He told of having found evidence of a pick, a mule shoe, various scraps of iron, and the cedar posts of a corral.]

Cold and Windey—So that the two men kept out as gard With the Horses—Was like to frees—as We Have kept two men garding the Horses all night Ever Since We left our House on the River and Intend keeping them up till We Rech the Spanish Settlement We this day maid fifteen miles—

Sunday [Monday] 4th Feby 1822

the Wind High and Very Cold We set out Early up the valley [139] a little West of South for about two miles thence up the Point of a mountain and along a Ridge leave High Peeks on both Sides till We took up a High Hill and threw a Pine groave Whar the Snow is three feet deep—and at about five miles from Camp We Came to the top or Backbon of the mountain Which devides the Watters of the arkensaw from the Delnort Heare the Wind Was So Cold We Scarce dare look Round—

South 5 miles to the top of the mountain [140]

We then Steered more West down the mountain to a branch [141] of

[139] Of the Huerfano river, which, if followed up W., would take him into Huerfano Park, between the Wet Mountain range and the Sangre de Cristo range.

[140] Making the Sangre de Cristo Pass, from the watershed of the Huerfano to that of the Rio Grande del Norte. See Pike, ed. of 1895, p. 492. It may be difficult or impossible to find the record of any earlier passage of these mountains by an American party, or indeed any previous itinerary of the whole Taos Trail.

[The trail taken by Fowler and his guides (and presumably by Glenn and Peno with the Spaniards a month earlier) was not the route of the Denver and Rio Grande Railroad and the modern highway through La Veta Pass, but one that lay slightly farther north. They followed the Huerfano River into the mountains (the Sangre de Cristo on their left and the Wet Mountains on the right) and turned southwest from that stream to climb the ridge between Oak Creek and South Oak Creek. When they had crossed the summit of this pass, they entered a canyon that led down and then over another ridge into the head of Pass Creek Canyon and emerged from it (at an elevation of slightly over 9,400 feet) through Sangre de Cristo Pass into the upper valley of Sangre de Cristo Creek. No record of an ealier crossing by this route has been found, although Spanish authorities were clearly acquainted with it. This route was probably that taken by Lieutenant John D. Albert in January 1847 when he was escaping to the north and by the 7th U.S. Infantry traveling south from Utah to New Mexico in the spring of 1860. Pike had crossed these mountains by way of what is now known as Medano Pass. Hart and Hulbert, *Zebulon Pike's Arkansaw Journal*, pp. 165–66; Jackson, *Journals of Zebulon Montgomery Pike*, I, 373 n.; and LeRoy R. Hafen, "John D. Albert," in Hafen, *Mountain Men and the Fur Trade of the Far West*, II, 21–26.]

[141] Sangre de Cristo creek, tributary to Trinchera creek, a branch of the Rio Grande. See Pike, ed. of 1895, p. 494.

the delnort—and down that about South for nearly ten miles to Wheare the mountains are much lower Whear [we] Capted [camped] for the [night] We Hear find no timber but Piny and Roal Some old logs off the mountain for fier Wood—Dick Walters is mising and on Inquirey He Had lost His Blanke[t]s Comeing down the mountain and tyed His Hors to a tree and gon back to find them and that His Hors broke loos and overtook the Reer party at about four miles from Whare He tied Him the Hors Was Hear Caut and tied again it is now Sundown and no Word of Dick We are afraid He is frosen   We maid fifteen miles this day—Walters got to Camp Some time In the night

S° 45 West 10 miles [142]

Monday [Tuesday] 5th Feby 1822
Set out Early down the Crick nearly South at five miles [leaving] the Crick on our Right Hand Came to Crick [143] Runing West With Some Cottenwood and Willows We Crossed this Crick Into an oppen plain [144] of great Exstent We Have now left the mountains behind us and on our left Hand tho there are Some to be Seen at a great distance on our Right and In frunt—our Cors is now South and Crossing a Small Crick at three miles and at twelve miles farther Camped on a Crick [145] 40 feet Wide full of Running Watter Some Cotten Wood trees and Willows We this day maid twenty one miles—South 21 miles

tusday [Wednesday] 6th Feby 1822
Set out the Sun about one Hour High nearly South along the mountains leave them on our left and pasing Some Small mounds [146] on the Right Which Stand alone in the Pirarie at fifteen miles Crosed

[142] Besides the distance above given for making the pass to-day. Camp on Sangre de Cristo creek, which flows past Fort Garland into Trinchera creek, in the San Luis valley. That branch of the D. and R.G.R.R. which goes through the Veta pass follows down the creek on which Fowler is camped.

[143] Trinchera creek. Fowler seems to have left Sangre de Cristo creek at a point about 4 m. E. of Fort Garland.

[144] A portion of the San Luis valley, through which the Rio Grande flows for a great distance. See Pike, ed. of 1895, p. 492.

[145] Rio Culebra, next tributary of the Rio Grande from the E. See Pike, ed. of 1895, p. 494.

[146] The San Luis hills, on each side of the Rio Grande near the Rio Culebra.

a Small Crick [147] Runing West from the mountains a Cross the plain and In the Evening Crossed two more Small Streems Runing as before and at night Camped on a Small Crick at the lower Eand of this large [San Luis] vally Heare the mountain Puts a Cross the Plain to the River Delnort about 6 miles to our Right as We Have been going down that River at about the above distance Ever Since We Came in to this plain—on this Crick there Is a Small Spanish vilege but abandoned by the Inhabetance for feer of the Indeans now at War With them We this day troted the Horses more than Half the time and maid thirty miles nor did We Stop till In the night

South 30 miles—

Wensday [Thursday] 7th Feby 1822

We Set [out] at an Early Hour Crossing a Crick [148] Well adapted for mills of Ither the Saw or the grinding and plenty of tall Pitch Pine— We Heare proceded up the Side of a High mountain and Continueing alonge the Side of it the River Runing Close under the futt of it So that the Was no other Way to pass—We Continued over Ruff grounds and deet guters for nine miles to a Small vilege [149] on a Crick— Heare We Capped [camped] in the vileg for the night—and our gides left us as Well as the Intarpreter after Shewing us Into a Hous as He Said of Honest People—and telling on ordors that I Had no money but wold pay in Such artickels as We Had the land lord Was verry Kind I obtained Some taffe [150] for the men as the Have not

[147] Rio Costilla, next tributary of the Rio Grande from the E. See Pike, ed. of 1895, p. 494. On reaching lat. 37° N. Fowler passes from Colorado into New Mexico. The principal landmark is Ute peak, isolated in the plain, a little south of the boundary and of Rio Costilla, on the E. bank of the Rio Grande, alt. about 10,000 feet.

[148] Apparently Colorado creek, another tributary of the Rio Grande from the E.

[149] San Cristobal—or the next village below, Los Montes. The "deet guters" of the text are the arroyos which Fowler intended to call deep gutters.

[About three miles below San Cristobal was the site on which Simon Turley later built a mill and a distillery. When the revolt against American occupation broke out in 1847, Turley's mill was one of the points attacked. Seven Americans, including Turley himself, were killed after a two-day siege. John Taylor Hughes, *Doniphan's Expedition* (Cincinnati, 1848), p. 393.]

[150] See Lewis and Clark, ed. of 1893, p. 215, for a similar name of ardent spirits, apparently the same word as *ratafia*. What Fowler procured was aguardiente de Taos, a fiery fluid distilled at San Fernandez from native wheat, and soon too/well known as "Taos lightning."

tasted any Sperits Since We left the virdegree He put all our goods in a dark Room and locked them up—and We lodged in an outer Room—the Inturpreter and guide promised us to Return to us Early—S° 30 West 9 miles

thorsday [Friday] 8th Feby 1822

We Had the Horses up Early and With Some defequeelty got out the Saddles and Bridles—and then atempted to Settle the Bill but the Spanierd Ither Cold not or Wold not under Stand me I Soposed the amt about Six dollers—and layed ten Dollers Worth of Knives and tobaco—Which He took up and put a Way I demanded the goods but to no purpose He Wold not let me Have them Still Saying that Battees[151] told Him not to let the goods go till He Came now this Battees Was one of the men Imployed Heare and Sent by Conl glann to asist us over the mountain—and I began to ConClude that Some vilenus Skeem Was at Worke betwen Him and the landlord as He did not Return as He promised—but after about three Hours disputeing and Indevering to get the goods I Seen that nothing but force Wold do I Steped to my gun and So did Robert Fowler I told the men to do the Same—and [when] I Seen all Readey I Spoke loud Saying I Wold Have the goods and Shoing much anger—the Spanierd got in a better umer and gave up the goods—So We loaded and moved on Crossing a Crick Which Run West threw the village

---

[*Aguardiente*, a kind of brandy, was also distilled from grapes in the El Paso, Texas, region. This liquor was known to Americans as Pass Whiskey. In 1825, James Baird, Samuel Chambers, Thomas ("Peg-Leg") Smith, and a man named Stevens established a distillery near Taos where they produced a corrosive and highly intoxicating drink known as Taos Lightning. Gregg, *Commerce of the Prairies*, p. 273; Dorothy Gardiner, *West of the River* (New York: Thomas Y. Crowell, 1941), p. 56; and Garrard, *Wah-To-Yah and the Taos Trail*, p. 206.]

[151] Baptiste Roy, the interpreter, who had gone on to Santa Fé with Col. Glenn.

[Both the way in which Fowler identified the man and the circumstances of the controversy imply that "this Battees" from whom the Spanish landlord in San Cristobal said he had received instructions was not Baptiste Roy, Peno, Moran, or Glenn's boy (all of whom had accompanied Fowler from the Verdigris), but another man, probably the "Inturpreter" Fowler had mentioned the previous evening. He may reasonably be identified with the "french Indean or Half Breed that Spoke the Cro language" whom Fowler mentioned on January 28. When Fowler had last mentioned Roy, on November 25, and when he wrote next, twice, on February 10, he wrote "Mr. Roy." Glenn, on December 29, also wrote "Mr. Roy." Their tone was always respectful.]

Steered a little South of East about twelve miles over a High Butifull plain to the villege of St Flander [152]—In the nibor Hood of touse.[153] about two miles from the villege We meet With Conl glann at the Crossing of a Crick[154] Which [ran] West—on our a Rivel at the villege We mised one of the Hors loads of meet and on Inquiery it was found that one of the Spanierds Head taken it of to His own Hous at about three miles distance   So We lost it there being no moad of Recovering it—He was one of the men Sent out to asist us over the mountains and that morning With out being notised put the load on His own Hors—and falling behind maid His Eskape With the meet—We Heare found the people extremly poor. and Bread Stuff Coud not be Head amongst them as the Said the grass hopers

152 San Fernandez de Taos, the Mexican village about 2 m. from the Indian Pueblo de Taos. Gregg states that the first white settler was a Spaniard named Pando, *ca.* 1745. See Pike, ed. of 1895, p. 598.

[Elsewhere the first white settler in the Taos Valley is identified as Pablo Villapando, whose daughter Maria Rosa was taken captive by the Comanches in a raid on Taos in August 1760. She was ransomed in 1770 and taken to St. Louis, where she married Jean Baptiste Salle, who was known as Lajoie (Sabin, *Kit Carson Days*, I, 26). Spanish settlers are also said to have come to Taos as early as 1615. When the Indians objected to their settling on the edge of the pueblo, the Spaniards moved a short distance away and established the present village of Taos. George I. Sanchez, *Forgotten People: A Study of New Mexicans* (Albuquerque: University of New Mexico Press, 1940), p. 44.

Fowler's "villege of St. Flander" is San Fernandez de Taos, the modern town of Taos, seat of Taos County. It is mentioned again as "St flander" on May 1, and as the "vilege" on May 31 and June 1. It is in this "villedge" that Glenn had his house. Fowler uses the name "touse" at this time and on May 1 to designate the Indian pueblo two miles away, but on March 8 "touse" probably means San Fernandez de Taos.]

153 Pueblo de Taos, the ancient seat of the Pueblo Indians of Taos, consisting then as now of two casas grandes—great adobe buildings with the streamlet between them. Readers who would like a little local color here will find it well laid on in chaps. xiii–xviii of Garrard's Wah-to-yah. The youthful author witnessed the executions which followed the battle of Taos in 1847.

[This pueblo was already old when Hernando de Alvarado saw it in 1540. The present site has been occupied since about 1700. The village consists of two groups of houses, five or six stories high, built on both sides of Taos Creek. It was one of the centers of Indian life and influence, and a focal point in the Pueblo Revolt of 1680. Later leaders of the pueblo participated actively in the revolt of 1847. Hodge, *Handbook of American Indians North of Mexico*, s.v. "Taos"; Sanchez, *Forgotten People*, pp. 43–86; and Stanley Stubbs, *Bird's-Eye View of the Pueblos* (Norman: University of Oklahoma Press, 1950), pp. 23–26.]

154 Pueblo creek, the northern one of two main forks of Taos creek.

Head Eat up all their grain for the last two years and that the Head to Pack all their grain about one Hunderd miles—for their own use— We found them Eaqually Scarce of meet and Ware offered one quarter of a doller a bound for the meet We Braght in With us—but this We Cold not spair and Haveing nothing Els to eat it Will not last us long—and no Bread Stuff to be got Heare We must Soon leave this Reeched place—and now in the dead of Winter and the Waters frosen tite Exsept the River Delnort Which is Said to be oppen to Which We Intend to go as Soon as poseble to Cetch Bever to live on as there is no other game In this part of the Cuntry—

Satterday 9th Feby 1822
Remained In the villedge all day and In the Evening there Was a Colletion [of the] men and Ladys of the Spanyerds   Had a fandango [155] in our House Wheare the appeered to InJoy them Selves With the Prest at their [head]—to a great degree—

[155] [Josiah Gregg describes the fandango as:

the usual designation for those ordinary assemblies where dancing and frolicking are carried on. . . . Nothing is more general, throughout the country, and with all classes than dancing. From the gravest priest to the buffoon— from the richest nabob to the beggar—from the governor to the ranchero— from the soberest matron to the flippant belle—from the grandest *señora* to the *cocinera*—all partake of this exhilirating amusement. To judge from the quantity of tuned instruments which salute the ear almost every night in the week, one would suppose that a perpetual carnival prevailed everywhere. The musical instruments . . . are usually the fiddle and *bandolin*, or *guitarra*, accompanied in some villages by the *tombé* or little Indian drum. The musicians occasionally acquire considerable proficiency in the use of these instruments. (Gregg, *Commerce of the Prairies*, p. 170)

Pike had also commented on the fandango (March 1, 1807). Jackson, *Journals of Zebulon Montgomery Pike*, I, 387.

At this time the mayor of Taos was Don Antonio Severino Martinez. His son Antonio Jose Martinez had gone to study at the seminary in Durango in 1817 and was ordained there on February 10, 1822, but did not return to his native village until January 1823. For many years afterwards he was famous as "the jolly priest of Taos" (and he became one of New Mexico's most distinguished citizens). The spirit he expressed was already clearly an important element in Taos life. A census of the town taken in December 1821, a month before Glenn's arrival, showed a population of 753 Indians and 1,260 Spanish and other inhabitants. Blanche C. Grant, *When Old Trails Were New: The Story of Taos* (New York: Press of the Pioneers, 1933); Antonio J. Martinez, "Apologia of Presbyter Antonio J. Martinez," *New Mexico Historical Review*, III (October 1928), 329; and Henry R. Wagner, "New Mexico Spanish Press," *New Mexico Historical Review*, XII (January 1937), 3–6.]

Sunday 10th Feby 1822

Remained In the villege all day But Sent out two parteys of trapes [156] to Remain out till the first of may next—Hear it may be Remembered that a Capten and and Sixty men of the Spanierds Came in from the arkensaw With Conl glann and little party—and now the Same Capten and party Has Crossed the mountaines again—but before He let [left] Home Has Interdused Conl glann and Mr. Roy to His family Consisting a Wife and two daughters both young Woman the old lady Haveing paid us a visid In the morning appered In a few minet quite formiler and as Well aquainted With us as If She Head knone us for several years tho She did not Stay more than about Half an Hour—But in the after noon a boy Came With a mesege for Conl glann mr Roy and the negro. Who after Some Ceremony acCompanyed the two gentlemen but With Some Reluctance aledgeing that He Was not Settesfyed to go With out His master aledgeing as the ladys appeerd more atached to Him than [to] the White men—that there might be Some mischeef Intended and uder those doupts He Went as I before Stated and from the Statement of those two gentlemen I Will Indevour to State What followed—it Is a Custom With the Spanierds When Interdused to Imbrace With a Close Huge—this Cermoney So Imbareshed Pall and maid Him So Shaimed that I [if] a Small Hole Cold Have been found He Wold Sartainly Crept Into it. but unfortnetly there Was no Such place to be found. and the trap door threw Which the desended Into the Room being Shut down [for the Went In at the top of the House] [157] there Was no Poseble Way for Him

---

156 [Within the next two days the expedition was divided into four trapping parties. One, led by Fowler himself, included Robert Fowler, Taylor, Walters, and Paul; a second was led by Jesse Van Bibber, and a third by Isaac Slover. The fourth, whose leader is not named, is called the "french partey" (May 1). Fowler's entry for March 1 seems to imply that Van Bibber's party numbered at least four men; it was later joined by Ward and Douglas. Glenn (and probably Roy) presumably remained at San Fernandez de Taos. If the French party included Bono, Barbo, Peno, and Moran, three of the four remaining men (Pryor, Simpson, Maxwell, and Findlay) would have been trapping with Van Bibber and one of them with Slover. Fowler records very little information about their assignments.]

157 Square brackets in the original MS.

[Entrance to common Mexican houses was gained by using an outside stairway or ladder leading to the roof, where a trap door gave access to the rooms below. There were no outside doors, and windows were small. Houses were built in this

to make His Escape—now the Haveing but one Beed in the House and that So large as to be Cappeble of Holding the three Copple of poson—there Ware all to lodge to geather and the mother of the daughters being oldest Had of Corse the ferst Chois of Bows. and took pall for Hir Chap takeing Hold of Him and drawing Him to the beed Side Sot Him down With Hir arms Round His Sholders. and gave Him a Kis from [?] Sliped Hir Hand down Into His Britches—but it Wold take amuch abeler Hand than mine to discribe palls feelings at this time being naturly a little Relegous modest and Bashfull He Sot as near the wall as Was Poseble and it may be Soposed He Indevoured to Creep Into it for Such Was His atachment to the old lady that he kept His [eyes] turned Constently up to the trap door—and to His great Joy Some person oppened it to Come In to the Same Room—But Pall no Sooner Saw the light [for their Rooms are dark] 158 than He Sprang from the old lady and Was out In an Instant—and maid to our lodgeing as fast as Poseble Wheare the other two Soon followed and told What Head Happened to Pall

monday 11th Feby 1822
Remained in the vilege all day nothin meterel took place.

tusday 12th Feby 1822
I Set out on a traping tower With Robert Fowler—Taylor Walters and Pall With Eight Horses 159 We Went South West about ten miles to the bank of the River [Rio Grande]—Which Bank or Bluf Was So High We Cold see no Chance of getting down With the Horses for We looked some time before We Cold see the River the distance Was So great 160—and the River looked like a Small Spring Branch that a man might Easely Step over—and Head We not been told that the River Was In that gap We Cold not Have beleved the River Was there at all—We then Pased down a long the Bluf about two miles and found a path Way down the mountain—the Bluf or

---

manner to provide protection against Indians. Lansing B. Bloom, ed., "The Rev. Hiram Walter Read Baptist Missionary to New Mexico," *New Mexico Historical Review*, XVII (April 1942), 125–27.]

158 Square brackets in the original MS.

159 [With the departure of Fowler the entire expedition was now engaged in trapping, except Glenn, Ward, and Douglas, and perhaps Roy.]

160 [Fowler was now traveling along the deep, tortuous canyon of the Rio Grande. It extends south from a point about ten miles below Fort Garland, Colorado, for approximately sixty miles.]

River Bank as you may Chose to Call it Which path We took but With great danger to our Horses and In about two Hours going down that mountain We got to the River Which is about one Hunderd yds Wide and is fordable With Horses—and now takeing a vew of the River I find it is at least one thousand feet below the leavel of Pirarie. and is bound With a bluf of Rocks on Each Side mostly Parpendickeler So that there Is but few plases that Ither man or Beast asend them—We are now at the mouth of the [Taos] Crick Which Pases threw touse Heare is two Houses With Each one family of Spanierds and it is not Poseble the Have more than Half an acer of ground to live on. and Shold a Rock Breake loos and Come down Wold destroy the Hole Settlement

S° 45 West 10 to the River

Wensday 13th Feby 1822

Robert Fowler and my Self Went down the River about Six miles on foot to look for Bever no Sign of any the River is So bound With Rocks that With much difequaty We maid our Way Heare We found a nother Small villege [161] With Eight or ten Houses and a foot Bridge a Cross the River over Which We Went and Heare We found a Path up the River Hills Which [were] full as High as Wheare We first Came to it But Heare the Rocks are So broken that a Papth Way is found up threw them after a long and tedeous Walk We a Rived at the top of the Hil and found our Selves on oppen leave[l] Pirarie of from forty to fifty miles Wide. We are now on the West Side of the River and Went up along the Bluf about two miles and Came to a dry Crick Which put into the River but the Rocks Ware So High on Each Side that We Walked up it about one Hour before We found any Poseble Chance of Crossing it after Which We pased over the leavel Pirarie opset our Camp [162] Wheare We found a path leading down threw the Rocks to the River and it appeers that there is no poseble Chance of going up or down these Clifts but at those paths—for as Soon as you Come to the top of these Clifts and look down you are so struck With Horror that you Will Retret In an Instant

thorsday 14th Feby 1822

Crosed the River Early and Wound up the mountain along a path

[161] Cieneguilla—to be distinguished from a place of the same name S. W. of Santa Fé.

[162] On Feb. 12, at the mouth of Taos creek.

maid By the Spanierds among the Rocks till We arived at the top in the oppen World and Steereing to the north leaving the River on our Right Hand and Camped at night opesed the villege Wheare We Head the defequeelty Withe the land lord We this day maid about fourteen miles[163]—and found no Watter for our Horses Sent two Kittles down to the River for Watter Heare We find the mountain about the Same Hight as Wheare We Ca[m]ped last night With a path up threw the Rocks maid by the People of the villege on the East side—

14 miles

Friday 15th Feby 1822

We Set out Early up the margin of the River about twelve miles to the point of a mountain Cut off by the River forming a parpendickelor Bluff of about fifteen Hunderd feet High—over this mountain We Head to Clime on the top of Which the Snow Was nee deep—tho there Was none on the Pirarie We Went four miles farther and Camped on the margen of the River Sent down two kittles for Watter and sot two bever traps—Heare the Rocks or Bluffs are a little Broken and not quite so High as Wheare We Stayed the two nights past—tho Heare they are about nine Hunderd feet High and So Steep—Exsept the Spot Wheare Sent down the kittles that a Squerel Cold not Climb them—our distance this day is Sixteen miles—16 miles

Satterday 16th Feby 1822

found one Bever in a trap this morning Sott the two traps again and moved up the River about Six miles and Ca[m]ped on the margen of the River the Rocks not So High as last night but So Steep that We Cold not git Watter from the River and melted Snow for that Purpose Which We found among Some Rocks We found some dry Ceders for fier Wood—6 miles

Sunday 17th Feby 1822

Very Cold Haveing Snowed a little In the fore part of the night Sent for the two Bever traps—the River Had frosen over them So that We Caught nothing—Seen two men on Hors Back at a great distance Soposed to be Indeans—the Road off as fast as their Horses Cold Carry them—We this day Seen Six Wild Horses tho two of them

[163] See back, date of Feb. 8: 14 m. from the mouth of Taos creek would bring him about to Los Montes, but not to San Cristobal.

must Have been In Hands as their tails Ware Bobed Short—We find no game yet and our Stock of provetion Is nearly out—

monday 18th Feby 1822

We Sot out Early up the River and at about 12 miles Came to the upper Eand of the High Rocks [164] and going down a gradual decent three or four Hunderd yds Came to a low Bottom on the River the Bank being low not more than six or Eight [feet] High the River butifull and a bout one Hundred yds Wide—But all frosen up tite— We Heare got Watter for the Horses—it Is Heare proper to Remark that the River as far as We Have Seen it pasing down betwen the High Rocks or mountains—dose not move In a very gentle manner as It appeers much Impeded by the Rocks falling from Each Side. and is forsed forward dashing from one Rock over others In almost one Continued foam the Hole distance threw the mountains Which from What I Can larn is about seventy miles When it appeers below In an oppen Cuntry—I Have no doubt but the River from the Head of those Rocks up for about one Hundred miles Has once been a lake of about from forty to fifty miles Wide and about two Hunderd feet deep—and that the running and dashing of the Watter Has Woren a Way the Rocks So as to form the present Chanel—We this day Crosed a dry Branch. But Have not Seen one Streem of Watter In all the distance We Have Came up on the [west] Side We travled nor Cold our Horses get one drop of Watter in all that distance but the Eat Snow When the Cold get it—We Went up the River a bout Six miles further and Camped on the East Side in a Small grove of Cotten Wood trees the Ice In [is] now so Strong the Horses Can Cross at pleasure—We find nothing to kill Exsept two of the Big Horned Sheep [*Ovis montana*] one of Which Robert Fowler shot but Cold not git it—

We this day maid Eighteen miles our Corse about north all the Way up the River—North 54 miles [165]

[164] Fowler has come by his count 48 m. from the mouth of Taos creek, N. along the right or W. bank of the Rio Grande, which runs in a cañon the whole of this way. This distance is about right to take him past the several special elevations between which and the river he passes, known as Cerros Taoses, San Cristobal, Montoso, Chifle, and Olla; when he reaches the low ground of which he speaks, there are a crossing of the river, cattle ranch, etc. See Pike, ed. of 1895, pp. 597, 598.

[165] That is, from the mouth of Taos creek to present camp—and this is about right for the vicinity of Ute peak, on the E. side of the Rio Grande, 4 m. S. of the boundary of Colorado (lat. 37° N.)

tusday 19th Feby 1822

We Set out Early up along the West Side of the River and at two miles Came to High Short Hills Which Put In Cloce to the River on both Sides and Continu for about three miles Wheare We find Wide and low Bottoms—Heare We See timber a Head Wheare We Will Indevour to Camp this night—and at ten miles We Came to Slovers party In Camped about two miles up Pikes forke of the Delnort [166] and about three miles below His Block House Wheare He Was taken by the Spanierds—this fork Is oppen ocationed by the large Warm Spring Spoken of In Pikes Jurnal this party Has Caught Some Bever and their Is Sign of more in the River our Cors this day Was north 30 West ten miles—there is plenty of Cotten Wood trees and Willowes along this but Scarce a tree on the main River

N 30 West 10 miles [167]

[166] [Fowler is now back in the area that became Conejos ("Rabbit") County, Colorado, and on the Conejos River. The stream rises in the San Juan Mountains in the central western part of the county. It flows southeast to the town of Canon, then turns northeast, and enters the Rio Grande three miles northeast of La Sauses. Here Lieutenant Pike built his stockade in 1807. Pike was born in New Jersey in 1779 and entered the army at an early age. In 1805–1806 he led an exploring expedition up the Mississippi River in search of its sources. On July 6, 1806, he set out on another journey of exploration into the far West in search of the headwaters of the Red and Arkansas rivers. He went up the Missouri and Osage rivers and across Kansas to the Arkansas, which he reached at the Great Bend. Continuing west along that river, he reached the foot of the Rocky Mountains and in November discovered the lofty peak that bears his name. After exploring parts of eastern Colorado, he entered the mountains by way of the Royal Gorge of the Arkansas and crossed the Sangre de Cristo Mountains to the upper headwaters of the Rio Grande in the San Luis Valley. At the junction of the Rio Grande and the Conejos River he built the stockade mentioned by Fowler. There on February 24, 1807, he and his party were seized by Captain Facundo Melgares (later the governor of New Mexico) and taken first to Santa Fe and later to Chihuahua for questioning. They were returned to the United States by way of San Antonio and Nacogdoches, Texas.]

[167] Neither this course nor this distance would bring Fowler to the Rio Conejos from any point on the Rio Grande to which the previous mileages appear to have advanced him. The distance is 15 m. on an air line due N. along the meridian of 105° 45′ from Myer's or Colona's ferry to the mouth of the Rio Conejos; hence we infer that Fowler has come up the Rio Grande further than his previous mileages would indicate. But there is no doubt, from his description in the above interesting passage, that he is on the Rio Conejos; and 2 m. up it would be 3 m. below Pike's stockade of 1807, as he says. See Pike, ed. of 1895, p. 495 and following, and p. 595.

Wensday 20th Feby 1822

We moved up the River threw the Bottom Which is about fifty miles Wide In Cluding the second Bottom leavel and Rich and not a tree to be Seen Exsept a few along the River bank—We maid twelve miles. and Camped on the East Side among Some Willows and geathered drift Wood for our fier—the Weather Is very Cold the Snow fell last night about two Inches deep—Cors north 12 miles[168] See nothing to kill

thorsday 21st Feby 1822

Crosed over on the Ice and up the West Side of the River the timber and Brush Is now plenty In the low bottoms Which are from two to four miles Wide tho these are not all Covered With timber—and Hear there Is on both Sides What We Call a second bottom a little Higher than the first—the Hole now makeing a distance of from 30 to 40 miles now Since We Have Came to the timber We find much Sign of Bever—But the River Is So frosen that We Cannot ketch them   We Camped on the East Side of the River and Conclude to go to the West mountains[169] In the morning and try to kill meet to Eat as our provetions are all gon—nor Have We Seen any kind of game Since We left Slovers party N 45 West 18 miles

Friday 22nd Feby 1822

Robert Fowler and my self Set out Early on futt for the West mountains and Steered for a Small streek of Brush Whear We Exspect to find Watter as that kind of Brush dos not grow With out We on the Way See Eight[y] or 90 Wild Horses and In devour to git In Shot distance so as to kill one to Eat—but In that We failed for Whin We Ware at about one miles distanes the Seen us and all Run off—We Went to the mountain and Camped by the Side of a large Rock Wheare We [found] both Wood and Watter Was plenty but nothing to Eat Pall and taylor Came up With the Horses We all Went up the mountains to Hunt But See nothing to kill—but there

[168] Passing La Jara and Alamosa creeks between 4 and 6 m. from the Rio Conejos. One of these, probably La Jara, is called Willow creek on April 28, p. 110.

[They turned west three or four miles above the site of the town of Alamosa.]

[169] The San Juan range of mountains, bounding the San Luis valley on the W., whence the Rio Grande issues into that valley in the vicinity of the place called Del Norte.

[The Rio Grande enters the San Luis Valley fifteen miles west of Del Norte at South Fork, a town that was not in existence in 1898.]

THE JOURNAL OF JACOB FOWLER

Was Some Sign of the Big Horned Sheep on the Sides of the mountain amongst the Short Pine Which Is plenty Heare In Some plases—the Weather Is Cold and Some flying Clouds—our Corse Was this day West 12 miles—We Heare found by going up the mountain the Snow Was So deep We Cold not travel tho there Was little or none In the valey

West 12 miles [170]

Satterday 23rd Feby 1822

We Conclude to go to the River and up it till We find game—Pall and my Self take the Horses and Steerd north to the River about ten miles Robert Fowler and Taylor out on the Hunt—Camped on the West Side of the River—nothing killed this day—

north 10 miles [to] West Side of the River [171]

Sunday 24th Feby 1822

nothing to Eat—Taylor Purposes to take Robert Fowlers Hors and Ride Hunting Which Was agread to He Went on the West Side of the River I Went my Self on the East Side up the River about ten miles to the Short Hills Seen Some Caberey but killed nothing Taylor did not Return at night—nothing to Eat but look at Each other With Hungrey faceses

[170] Fowler has fetched up against the San Juan range somewhere about the foot of Pintada peak, whence creeks called Piedra Pintada, San Francisco, and others, flow E. and N. into the Rio Grande. The above "large rock" is Hanging Rock on p. 105.

[Hanging Rock is a high bluff on the north bank of the Rio Grande opposite Del Norte, Colorado.]

[171] In the vicinity of La Loma del Norte, Rio Grande Co.

[The town of Del Norte. On this day's march they passed opposite the mouth of Embargo Creek, which rises in the La Garita Mountains about fifteen miles to the northwest, at the foot of Mesa Mountain. John Charles Frémont's pitiable expedition withdrew painfully down this stream after its disaster at the head of Wannamaker Creek in December 1848 and January 1849. The Frémont party sought a pass for a railroad to the Pacific coast at the instigation of a group of businessmen in St. Louis and had the picturesque "Old Bill" Williams as a guide. They lost their entire pack train of 120 mules, baggage, and camp equipment, and eleven of thirty-two men perished from cold and hunger. Williams lost his own life in this area a few weeks later. Irving Stone, *Men To Match My Mountains* (Garden City, N.Y.: Doubleday, 1956), pp. 124–29; and Alpheus Favour, *Old Bill Williams, Mountain Man* (Chapel Hill: University of North Carolina Press, 1936).]

monday 25th Feby 1822

this morning Taylor Came Into Camp on futt Haveing lost the Hors
With Sadle Bridle Blankets nek Roap and all In the first Short Hills
on the West Side of the River at Some ten or twelve miles up—and
that He Said He Head Seen many deer Elk and Bares—to Which
place We moved as fast as poseble and got there about 3 oclock Seen
a great many deer but killed nothing—our Corse West ten miles

tusday 26th Feby 1822

all out and Hunt till about 10 oclock but killed nothing tho Seen Some
deer—We now begin to think of killing one of our Horses—but first
move to a fresh Camp Wheare We Have not disturbed the game and
try In the Evening again to kill Something We move about two miles
to the River—as We Were now Camped on a Small Crick[172]—and
put out the Horses Robert and my Self took our guns to Hunt on
futt as there Was much timber land Heare—but Taylor and Pall
Began to Complain of Hunger of Which Taylor began gro black In
the face and Pall Was gitting White With the Same Complaint and
the both thaught the Hors Shold be killed. to Which Robert and my
Self Consented and gave them liberty to kill Him as Soon as the
Cold—but not Willing to See that operation Robert and my Self
Went off to Hunt but We Soon Heard the gun fier that We Soposed
to kill the Hors—but We kept our Corse down the River on the Ice
as the Brush Was thick and dry So that If We Went on land We maid
So much nois that We Could not git neer the game—but We Head
not gon far before Som deer Was Seen In the Brush and Robert
Went after them and killed two of them He then Went to Camp for
a Hors leaveing me to take Care of the deer—but When He got to
Camp He found one of the Horses about Half Skined—but another
Was Soon got up and the deer Caryed to Camp Wheare We Soon
Head Suntious feest and much Plesentness now appeered Round the
fier tho We lamented the fate of the Poor Hors—as now [we] Head
no use for His flesh Which feel a pray to the Birds and Wolves

Wensday 27th Feby 1822

Sent Pall out Early to look for the Horses We Soon Heard the
Report of gun and not long after Pall Came In With a deer on His
back the first He Ever killed In His life—We Have meet plenty and

172 Perhaps Wolf creek, making down from Del Norte peak, or another in
that vicinity.

the Weather Is now moderate Some Holes appeer a longe Shore In the Ice out at Which the bever Workes We Sot some traps this day—

thorsday 28th Feby 1822

Caught one bever—and Hunted for the lost Hors—but Have not found Him—

Friday 1st march 1822

Taylor Caught one Bever—Hunted for the lost Hors—met With vanbeber and two of His party the had found our lost Hors—the Remained at our Camp that night the Hors Head lost all but the Bridle

Satterday 2nd march 1822

vanbeber and His Party Set out Early up the River We Con Clude to follow them one or two days Exspecting We may find Some Elk— We Went up the [River] twelve miles pasing at Seven miles a large pond of Watter of about 40 acers on the West Side of the River— the Bottom of Which is about one mile Wide the mountains High on Each Side—the tops of Which are a great Hight above vegatation at about ten miles We Crost a fork [173] Puting In on the West Sid about one third as large as the River it appeers to Head to the West— Heare the River makes a turn to the north as fare as We Cold See up it—We Camped With vanbebers party the Head killed one Elk—our Cors West 12 miles—Heare the mountains Put Close to the River Which [is] very Croked

Sunday 3rd march 1822

I Remained at Camp Robert [Fowler] and Taylor Went Hunting the formor killed two Elk and left the latter to butcher them While took out Horses and braught them In to Camp

monday 4th march 1822

Went up the River to look for Sign of Bever but found none

[173] This fixes the position of the party exactly. This is the South Fork of the Rio Grande, above which the main stream comes S. E. from Wagon Wheel Gap, for about 12 m. to the forks. Fowler's compass points are here far out; the Rio Grande is flowing about E. from the forks to the plains; and the courses of the two forks *from* their confluence upward are, respectively, about S. W. and N. W.

[Coues is correct. The two forks join a short distance below the village of South Fork, which is shown on older maps as Baxterville. Just below the junction and on the north side of the river is the mouth of Alder Creek. It was this stream that Frémont followed into the La Garita Mountains on his ill-fated expedition in 1848.]

tuesday 5th march 1822

We moved down the River to the first High point of Rocks on the East [north] Side at the Head of the large vally and about one mile below Where We killed the Hors—Some Snow fell last night the Weather Cold the River Is yet frosen up Close Except a few Springs in the River bank Which keeps it oppen a few feet—High Wind last night—

Wensday 6th march 1822

Sot Some traps—Taylor Came In late at night Reports that Some Indeans are Camped about Eight miles below us on the River

thorsday 7th march 1822

Taylor purposes going to the Indeans Camp I gave Him Some tobaco for that purpose—He Went to the Indeans Robert my Self and Pall Road out the mountains and on our Return We See a nomber of Indeans at Camp Which We Cold See at Some distance from the point of one of the mountains and not noing what Indeans the Ware we vewed them about Half an Hour—the then moved off from our Camp and We Came In—Wheare We found taylor—tho the Indeans Had Stolen two Buffelow Roabs Some lead and two knives— and Ware of the utaws nation [Utes] [174] Which Roame about and live In the mountains Without Haveing any Settled Home and live alltogether on the Chase Raising no grain—Slover With His party Pased up the River this day—

Friday 8th march 1822

We Remain at the Same Camp—Caught one Bever and one aughter

[174] [The Ute, or Utah, Indians of the historic period occupied the entire central and western portions of Colorado and the eastern part of Utah, including the eastern part of Salt Lake Valley and Utah Valley. On the south they extended into New Mexico, occupying much of the upper drainage area of the San Juan River. They were a warlike people, frequently in conflict with their neighbors. Between 1630 and 1640 the Utes associated with the Spaniards, from whom they soon obtained the horse. In consequence they moved out onto the Great Plains and became buffalo hunters. They spent their summers in the mountains of western Colorado and in the San Luis Valley and some of them also spent their winters in that area. In 1735, Don Juan Rivera, leader of an exploring expedition into western Colorado, came in contact with them, as did Fathers Escalante and Domingues in 1776. American penetration into Ute territory began in 1807 when Lieutenant Pike entered the San Luis Valley. Hodge, *Handbook of American Indians North of Mexico*, s.v. "Ute."]

[otter] Ward and duglass Came to our Camp from touse [Taos] [175]—
and State that the Spanierds Have Sent 700 men against the nabeho
[Navajo] Indeans [176]—and of a battle being faught between Spanierds
and the Panie Indeans [177] East of the mountains

Satterday 9th march 1822

Ward and Duglass Set out for vanbebers Camp—In the Evening two
Spanierds Came to Camp [178]—Hard frost last night

Sunday 10th march 1822

Went up the River above the forkes to kill meet the two Spanierds
With us—

monday 11th march 1822

We Hunted till 12 oclock for Elk but found none—We Continued up
the north [fork] about Eight miles Heare the mountains Close in on
both Sides So that our Pasege Was Defequal and the River turning
to the West—We maid ten miles and Camped With Slover and
vanbeber Partey the Have all meet Heare together—the Have killed
two Elk N° 8 miles—West 2 miles [179]

[175] [Eli Ward and George Douglas had evidently remained in Taos with Glenn
when the others went into the San Luis Valley to trap beaver.]

[176] [Early Spanish records mention these people as "Apaches de Nabaju."
Before historic times they migrated southward and were probably on the plains
of eastern New Mexico and western Texas before the middle of the sixteenth
century. Roving and predatory, they were intermittently at war with the Spaniards
and almost continually at war with the tribes of the Great Plains. Between the
fall of Spanish power in New Mexico and the American occupation they frequently raided the Mexican settlements for horses, cattle, and sheep. Their
stronghold, Canyon de Chelly, was captured by Colonel Kit Carson in 1863, but
fighting continued for many years beyond that date. Hodge, *Handbook of
American Indians North of Mexico*, s.v. "Apache."]

[177] [Occasionally the New Mexicans would raise a small nondescript body of
men and sally forth in pursuit of the raiding Navajos or other Indians. Poorly
armed with lances, lassos, and a few guns, the New Mexicans usually were
defeated.]

[178] [These Spaniards probably came up from Taos with Ward and Douglas.
See the entry for March 13.]

[179] Up the North Fork or main Rio Grande, in Wagon Wheel Gap, to a point
about 2 m. below the mouth of Hot Spring creek, presently mentioned in the text.

[At Wagon Wheel Gap, about twelve miles above the junction of the two forks,
the river flows through a narrow passage in a mountain spur. A motel, a dude
ranch, and the Denver and Rio Grande Railroad station are located there.]

tusday 12th march 1822

Robert and myself Set out Early to Hunt and Haveing been In-
formed that a Hot Spring [180] Had been found up the Crick Which put
In to the River from the West [south] Side a little above our Cam[p]
—We Went to the Spring about one and a Half miles up the Crick—
But the Smoke appeered like that of a Salt furnis—as Soon as We
Came In vew of it—the Snow Was now about Six Inches deep over
the valley of the Crick But the Hot Watter Head kept the ground
Cleane for a few Rods Round the Spring—but What appeered
Straing to look at Was to see Ice Exstended about three feet from
the Shore over the Watter—tho a boiling up In the middle of the
Pon[d] Which Was about three Rods a Cross and nearly Round
the Spert of Watter Rose up Some distance above the leavel of the
Watter In the Pon and Was about the Size of a flour Barrel—now
the question Was How Can the Ice Existe on Hot Watter. I Caught
hold of the Ice as I Soposed—and [was] not only Scalded With the
Watter but the [was] Burned With the Ice it being nearly as Hot as
the Watter—bout on a farther Examination I found it Was a
mineral Substan that Had Congeled on the Watter of Which there
Ware vast quantitys laying below the Spring In the Crick Which
Run from it—We then Went up the mountain till the Snow got So
deep We Ware obliged to Return—killed nothing—this forke [Hot
Spring creek] of the River Heads nearly [south] in the High mountains—the main River Heading north [181] and from appeerence the
mountains Seperates and be Comes Lower as you go up the River
leaveing a large valley—and low Bottoms along the River—the two
Spanierds tell us it is about one days travel to the Head of the River [182]
—the Cuntry is low a Crass to the arkensaw—about twenty miles
north [west] from Heare and Six East [north] of this River there Is a
large lake [183] or Bodey of Watter that Has no out let that there is

180 [This spring, around which another dude ranch has been built, is still
active, but apparently it is not so large as it was when Fowler saw it.]

181 About W. from Fowler's present position, and much further off than the
Spaniards told him.

182 [The Spaniards were right about the distance from Wagon Wheel Gap to
the head of the Rio Grande, which is about one day's travel. They were wrong,
however, in saying that the country from the latter place to the Arkansas River
is low; it is very rugged and high.]

183 Santa Maria lake, about in the position indicated, if we make the required
correction of compass points. This lake is 2 or 3 m. N. E. of San Juan City, a

Some Island In it With trees on them—the all So State that this lake lyes be twen the Delnort and the arkensaw and that the Cuntry is low all the Way betwen the two Rivers—

Wendsday 13th march 1822
We Heare left the two Spanierds With Slover as We Head Dick Walters at His Camp on Pikes fork We moved down the River a little below the main forkes and killed one Elk Wheare We Camped for the night—bothe the other partys pased us Heare and Camped about one mile below us—the Ice begins to thaw and all makeing for the Bever Sign—

thorsday 14th march 1822
this morning two of our Horses Ware mising—about twelve oclock We found them and moved down to Hanging [Rock] as We Have Called it at our old Camp—the Weather Has got Cold and the Ice Harder—We Will not be able to trap for Some time yet—We Heare find the flax [Linum perenne] In abondance the Rute Is purenal [root is perennial] but In Every other appeerence it is like ous—

Friday 15th march 1822
Remained In Camp—the Ice begins to thaw in the day time but Hard frost at night—

Satterday 16th march 1822
Remained in Camp all day—

Sunday 17th march 1822
Remained in Camp all day—

monday 18th march 1822
Some difequalty With Taylor He quits us or We leave Him—and move up a Crick [184] to the South a bout four miles to Some bever Dams—Robert Fowler Complains of the Sore throat for Some days— and is gitting Worse
    South 4 miles

---

place on the Rio Grande in Antelope park, at the mouth of Clear creek. The road from the Rio Grande N. W. to Lake fork of Gunnison river skirts Santa Maria lake, and strikes the Lake fork at San Cristobal lake.

184 [This was Pinos Creek.]

tusday 19th march 1822

Robert is Still Worse With the Sore throat—We apply a sock With ashes Round His neck—He finds Releef in about two Hours— Hard frost this morning and Cold With High Winds

Wensday 20th march 1822

Caught three Bever and Examin the Crick about Six miles Higher up to Wheare the mountains[185] Close In on both Sides there Is timber and Willows all along this Crick and the bottoms about Half a mile Wid and Well adopted for Cultavation on acoumpt of Eragation— as no other lands Can be Cultivated Heare for the Want of Seasnable Rains—

S° 30 W 6 miles

thorsday [Friday] 29th march 1822

We Have Remained Heare Waiting for the Ice to melt out of the Crick but the Weather Continues Cold and Clouday With frequent Snow Storms the Ice is Still frosen over the bever dams So that We Caught but few—Robert Sore throat Has gon much better—We moved down to the River about 3 miles above our old Camp killed three gees—Sot Some traps—the gees is now Coming plenty and those We killed fatt Which is pleasing to us as We Have now lived a long time on Poor meet—Cloudey and begins to Snow—the Ice is nearly gon out of the River

Satterday 30th march 1822

the Snow is about four Inches deep Caught one bever killed one Sand Hill Crain [*Grus mexicana*] and five gees—the day is Warm—the Snow all gon out of the valleys but the mountains are all Covered moved to down to the old Camp

Sunday 31st march 1822

Caught four Bever and killed five gees—the Weather is gitting Cold

monday 1st aprile 1822

Killed five gees—the Watter frose over the traps Caught no bever

tusday 2nd aprile 1822

Caught two bever—and Remained the ballence of the day In Camp

Wensday 3rd aprile 1822

Caught one Bever killed three gees—the Weather much Warmer We

185 [Near Pintada Mountain.]

move up the Crick to the Bever dams—find the Ice much thiner and Sot Some traps—

thorsday 4th aprile 1822

Hard frost last night and frose up the traps Caught but one bever We now find that In this Crick the Watter Rises by Suns thaw Ing the Ice and at night With the Hard frost so that the Rise and fall of the Watter will defeet the traping[186]

friday 5th aprile 1822

moved Early about East threw a low [gap] In the Spurs of the mountains about ten miles and Camped a little below the Spanish Road leading to Pikes [fork. In the] gap In the mountain—We Sot Some traps—N 70 East 10 to the River[187]

Satterday 6th aprile 1822

Caught one Bever—We find the River as Well as the Crick Rises In the day with melting of the Ice for it Cannot be the Snow In the mountain the distance up to the Snow prevents the Watter from Ever Retching the vally the ground is so dry and loose that the Watter all dis appeers before it Can Rech near the futt of the mountains and Haveing Had frost at night the River falls as much as it Rises in the day—Taylor Came to our Camp to day and States that there are a great many Indeans on the River both above and below us that the Had Robed His Camp and taken all His traps but that He Had followed them and got all back but two traps

Sunday 7th aprile 1822

Caught one Bever and moved down the River about 12 miles on the north Side   We Have killed twelve gees Since We Have been on the River last—

monday 8th aprile 1822

Caught one Bever—Killed five gees moved down the River to the

[186] [It is apparent that the expedition up to this time was a failure as far as beaver trapping was concerned. The men were in an untouched area and the animals were plentiful enough, but the streams and ponds were solidly frozen. With little prospect for an early improvement in conditions, and the time to start for home not far distant, Fowler may have considered abandoning the enterprise.]

[187] Text obscure, but intelligible if read as above amended. The trip was from the creek on which the party had trapped through a gap to the Rio Grande at a point whence the Spanish road led from the river down the west side of the San Luis valley to the Rio Conejos.

lower Eand of the timber—the Indeans are all gon to the West over the mountains the Ware the utaws nation—

tuesday 9th aprile 1822

moved down the River about ten miles—and then turned East across the valley to a crick [188] and up it about five miles—this Crick Heds to the north as Is the Same We Came down Where We Crosse the mountains In feby last—We this day mett With venbeber and Ward—

Wensday 10th aprile 1822

Heare Is Some Indeans from the Spanish Settlement—We moved up the Crick about ten miles lost one bever trap—N° 10 miles

thorsday 11th aprile 1822

Went up the Crick about three miles and found Some Sign of bever— Sot Some traps—We yesterday pased threw Some of the Richest bottom on the Crick that I have Seen and Contains Six or Eight thousand acers [189]

N 20 West 3 miles

friday 12th aprile 1822

Cold and Clouday the Crick frose up—We Caught nothing—We Set out threw the Pirarie down the Crick a Snow Storm Came on and Caught us In the Pirarie the Wind and Snow in our faces So that We Cold not See one another two Rods—this Storm lasted about two Hours and it Was Weel for us it Seesed for We Cold not See Which Way to go and our Setuation Was Realy unplesent—

We Camped near the mouth of the [Trinchera] Crick Wheare We found Some timber—

Satterday 13th aprile 1822

the ground is now Covered With Snow and Hard frosen—We Have not Seen one morning With out frost Since the Winter first Sot In— We Crossed the River a little above Pikes forke [Rio Conejos] and ConCluded to go back to the timber up the River [190] for Which We Steered for three or four miles and Crossed a large Streem [La Jara]

[188] Trinchera creek, whose Sangre de Cristo branch the party descended Feb. 4 and 5. See note 143.

[189] Vicinity of Fort Garland, Costilla Co., Col.

[190] [The weather having presumably moderated, Fowler decided to turn back upstream for one more attempt at trapping beaver. Entries in the journal indicate that his luck had changed for the better.]

of Runing Watter forty feet Wide and nearly beley deep to the Horses —We Head Crossed this Same Crick in febuy last [Feb. 20] but the Was no Watter then In it it Haveing to pass over about twenty miles of oppen leavel Pirarie it Was all frosen to Ice—at that time and Is now melted and Coming down—the Snow Has disappeered In the valey but the mountains Covered—

[Sunday, April 14th—no entry]

monday 15th aprile 1822
Caught 2 beve and killed one goos We yester day Seen our Hors lost by vanbebers Party but So willd We Cold not take Him—

tusday 16th april 1822
Caught one Bever and moved up the River about four miles and Camped on the West Side vanbebers party pased us on the East going up all So—

Wensday 17 aprile 1822
Caught one bever and moved up the River about 12 miles the day Cloudey and Cold Comesed Snowing fast In the Evening and Continued till late at night—

thorsday 18th aprile 1822
the Snow about Six Inches deep We Caught one Bever and killed four gees—the day Warm the Snow all gon before night—

Friday 19th aprile 1822
killed two gees and Caught two Bever—Remained the ballence of the day at Camp—

Satterday 20th aprile 1822
Caught 2 Bever and killed two gees the Weather Warm the grass begins to appeer a little moved up the River a bout Seven miles Seen about twenty Elk Robert Shot one but it went off With the Rest—the mountains are Still Covered With Snow tho none In the valeys—

Sunday 21st aprile 1822
Caught two bever killed one goos moved up the River about Six miles Seen nine Elk—

monday 22nd aprile 1822
Caught two bever killed one goos and moved up the River to the

Hanging Rock [191] and from that to the Bever dams on the Crick
Wheare We left on the 6th Instent Soposeing the Ice Wold be gon out
of the Crick—

tusday 23 aprile 1822

Caught two bever—the Weather Cold—no game Hear and the Bever
Poor We Will move to the River In the morning on acoumpt of
killing gees to Eat—

Wensday 24th aprile 1822

Caught two bever moved to the River and Crosed over to the East
Side and Camped a little below the Hanging Rock killed one goos
and one duck—

thorsday 25th aprile 1822

Caught one Bever killed one goos and moved down the river about
five miles—

Friday 26th april 1822

Set out down the River Intend to go to the Settlement We are
giting Scarce of Powder Haveing to Shute So much at gees for Want
of larger game—killed two Caberey and one Elk—maid Eight miles
and Camped on the East Side of the River—

Satterday 27th aprile 1822

killed two gees moved down the River near the lower Eand of the
timber Seen many Elk the Have now left the mountains and Come
Into the timber land on the River to feed on the young grass—

Sunday 28th aprile 1822

no frost this morning and the first We Have Seen this Spring—the
grass groes but Slow the trees not yet Buding the ground is as dry as
dust no moisture but the Snow Since We Came to the Cuntry and
the Spanierds Say that It is three years Since the Have Had Rain—
we moved down the River about four miles and Crossed to the West
Side of the River and Steered South at about ten miles Crosed the
Willow Crick and at about fifteen miles pased a Spring In the leavel
Pirarie Which Contained about on Hogset of Clear Cool Watter
Standing on Rise or mound of Earth a little above the leavel of the
Pirarie the ground Round this Spring Was quite Soft and Wen We
Ware at the Watter by Jumping on the ground you Cold See it

191 See back, date of Mar. 14, p. 105.

THE JOURNAL OF JACOB FOWLER

Shake for about two Rods all Round—about five miles farther We
Crosed Pikes forke at the mouth of the Warm Spring Branch Spoken
of by that gentleman In Jurnal [192] We then pased threw Some low
Hills a little East of South Seven miles to the River and Crossing over
found the Watter up to the Saddle Sceats and one of our Pack
Horses fell down with his load and Was not able to Rise So that We
Had Some difequalty to Keep Him from be drounded We then pased
over a low Ridge about Half a mile and Camped on a crick Wheare
We found Some Woods—

monday 29th aprile 1822

Clouday With High Winds Some Snow—We moved on Intending to
Camp on a branch With Some timber on the East Side of the Snake
Hill at twelve miles We maid the Branch but no Watter—We Went
up the the Crick about Eight miles and there found it a Bold Runing
Streem [193] Hear We Camped for the night makeing in [all] twenty
miles   We Seen Heare on this Crick a great many Cabery but very
Wild
    South 45 East 18 [sic] miles

tusday 30th aprile 1822

Hard frost the Ice about the 8th of an Inch on the kittle of Watter
Killed a Woolf at Camp—and Set out up the [Culebra] Crick to-
[ward] the mountains about three miles Whear We Struck the Road
to touse [Taos] Which We took and Camped at the Hords mans
villege but no purson to be Seen the Have deserted that place—about
Sundown Six Indeans Came to our Camp the Ware of the apacha
nation now at Pace With the Spanierds—the derected us to go off
Emedetly Saying that the utaws Had Stolen three Horses from our
men and that [they] Wold Steel ours if We Stayed at this place all
night—We geathered up our Horses and after night moved off about
three miles and lay Without fier—

[192] At p. 502 of the ed. of 1895; see also my notes at pp. 495, 496, for this Ojo
Caliente at the foot of the hill opposite Pike's stockade on the Rio Conejos. For
the above named Willow (La Jara) creek, see back, p. 108 and note 168, Apr. 13
and Feb. 20.

[193] Rio Culebra, which Fowler first passed Feb. 5, on his way to Taos: see
note 145. "Snake river" translates the Spanish name, and the "Snake Hill" of
the text is that one of the San Luis hills which is near this river, on the E. side of
the Rio Grande.

Wensday 1st may 1822

We Went down to St flander [San Fernandez de Taos] in the nibor Hood of touse [Pueblo de Taos] and find Conl glann Is gon to stafee [Sante Fé][194] We Remained Heare two days vanbebers Party Head Came In and the french partey[195] Is Heare all So—We now find all the Horses that ware left Heare very Poor and the Rainge near the vilege all Eat out I then ConCluded to take all the Horses out of the Settlement to good Rainge So as to fatten them or the Will not be able to to Cross the mountains on the first of June as that Was the time We In tend to Set out I therefore derected them all to be Collected and that I Wold move them In the morning.—

We Ware Informed that Spanish army[196] Had Returned that they Hag taken one old Indean and Some two or three old Horses that Ware So poor the Nabeho [Navajo] Cold not drive them up the mountains—for it appers the Went up the Steep mountain and Role down the Rocks on their Pursurs So that the Ware Compled to discontinu the pursute—

Satterday 4th may 1822

moved up the Crick South about five miles and Camped in the forks near Some Hords men Ho kept a large lot of Cattle from [whom] We obtained Some Cows milk We took With us 16 Horses—all We Cold find

Sunday 5th may 1822

Went up the East fork of the Crick about Eight miles—find the Bever Have been all taken out by Some trapers—the mountain is High and Steep and Croud Close to the Crick on both Sides We Returned to Camp Wheare Barbo and Simpson Had braught Eight more horses makeing in [all] twenty four—grass is Heare very good— the Horses Will Soon get fatt—this Evening Cloudey With thonder and a little Rain the first We Have Seen on this Side of the mountain

194 [After his first brief visit to Santa Fe in January, Glenn had settled down in Taos about the end of the month. Sometime after March 1, and probably after the middle of April, he rode to Santa Fe a second time, returning to Taos during the first week in May. About the middle of May it seems that he made a third brief trip to the provincial capital. Thomas James, *Three Years among the Indians and Mexicans*, ed. Walter B. Douglas (St. Louis: Missouri Historical Society, 1916), pp. 136–37, 157, 160, 161.]

195 [Probably Bono, Barbo, and others.]

196 [The "Spanish army" was undoubtedly the company mentioned in the entries of December 31, 1821, and February 10, 1822.]

monday 6th may 1822

Clouday and a little Rain—the Horses all Collected the are all poor but the grass is good and the Will thrive—I purchased a bull from a Spanierd for which I gave Him my great Coat and one knife—the Beef Was Prety good it Rained a little In the Evening

tusday 7th may 1822

Cool With flying Clouds and a little Rain Battess braught taylors mule to Camp Which He Head Reported to Have been Stolen by the Indeans Potter [197] Came to Camp With Conl glanns Horse He Has Returned from Stafee—

Wensday 8th may 1822

Hard frost the Horses all presend Went down to the vilege—We Heare that the Congrass Has Convened at maxeco—and that the Indeans Have taken a great many Horses from this niborhood and killed Some Cattle

thorsday 9th may 1822

Hard frost In the morning and Rained a little In the Evening

friday 10th may 1822

Cool With flying Clouds and High Wind—our Horses all present

Satterday 11th may 1822

Some flying Clouds and warm In the evening

Sunday 12th may 1822

Cloudey With flying Clouds—the trees giting green the Cotten Wood leaves Half gron[grown]—the People not yet don Sowing Wheat

monday 13th may 1822

flying Clouds and High Winds Continues Cloudey With lightning threw the night

tusday 14th may 1822

Clouday and Rain threw the day

Wensday 15th may 1822

the Snow from 4 to 5 Inches deep—Clers up about 10 oclock and Warm the Snow disappers in the vallys but Hangs on in the mountains

[197] New name, probably of some man who has joined the party. See June 1, p. 115, where James and McKnight's party join.

[Perhaps he was the Benjamin Potter in Thomas James's party. James, *Three Years among the Indians and Mexicans*, pp. 98, 197–99, 201, 206.]

thorsday 16th may 1822
Some frost In the morning but Warm after Sun Rise

friday 17th may 1822
flying Clouds and High Winds—

Satterday 18th may 1822
flying Clouds and High Wind

Sunday 19th may 1822
Cloudey and Warm for the Season

monday 20th may 1822
High Winds and Clouds—

tusday 21st may 1822
Clouday and Cool in the morning—High Winds about 12 oclock and
Continu till Sundown—

Wensday 22nd may 1822
Clouday and Winday—

thorsday 23rd may 1822
Cloudey With thonder like for Rain—Clears off In the after noon
With High Wind

friday 24th may 1822
flying Clouds and High Wind

Satterday 25th may 1822
the Wolves maid an atackt on our Horses the Wounded one Hors and
two mules We Have maid a Strong Pen Close to Camp and Still Shut
up all the Horses at night While We Remain at this place—to protect
them from the Wolfes—

Sunday 26th may 1822
Clouday and Warm all day—

monday 27th 1822
Clouday With High Winds and thonder Several thonder gust With
a little Rain in the night—

tusday 28th may 1822
Cool With High Winds and flying Clouds—Snow Storms In the
Evening—but light—

Wensday 29th may 1822

Cool With flying Clouds We are now makeing Some araingements for our Jurney over the mountains Some few days back Robert Fowler killed two young White Bares and braught them to Camp

thorsday 30th may 1822

Road down to the vilege all Hands prepairing to Set out on the first day of June for the United States—Clouday With thonder in the Evening—Some Rain in the night—the Snow Still Continu on the High mountains—

Friday 31st may 1822

Cool With flying Clouds and High Winds—the Horses all Collected and Sent to the vilege Except Except those for Robert my Self and pall—We Will go down In the morning—

Satterday 1st June 1822

Clear With White frost We Set out Early to Join the party at the vilege Wheare We found all Ready to Start—all So James and mcnights party from Stafee Had Joined ours and all moved on together [198] East four miles to the mountain—and there took up a

[198] The party start for home by a different route from that on which they came to Taos. Crossing the mountains eastward by the Taos Pass, they leave the watershed of the Rio Grande for that of the Arkansaw, and fetch out of the mountains on certain headwaters of the Canadian, as noted beyond.

In Gregg's Comm. of the Pra., i, 1844, p. 19 and p. 67 (quoted in Pike, ed. of 1895, p. 437), it is stated that a party of about a dozen men, including two named Beard and Chambers, reached Santa Fé in 1812, and returned to the U. S. in 1822. In Inman's Santa Fé Trail, p. 41, it is made eight years after James Pursley's trip that "Messrs. *McKnight*, Beard, and Chambers, with about a dozen comrades, started with a supply of goods across the unknown plains, and by good luck arrived safely at Santa Fé," where their troubles began; their wares were confiscated, and most of them were incarcerated at Chihuahua "for almost a decade." Inman agrees with Gregg that Beard and Chambers reached St. Louis in 1822, and notes that "McKnight was murdered south of the Arkansas by the Comanches in the winter of 1822," meaning of 1822–23. This McKnight is obviously the man whom Fowler names.

[Thomas James wrote in his recollections a quarter of a century later:

Most of my company had been engaged in trapping during my stay in Santa Fe, and some had gone far into the interior of Mexico. Collecting such as remained, and in company with the McKnights, I now, on the first of June, 1822, bade adieu forever to the capital of New Mexico, and was perfectly content never to repeat my visit to it or any other part of the country.

I started from Santa Fe with Hugh Glenn on his return to Taos, whence he was to go with me to St. Louis.

Crick [199] north 75 East aleven miles to the forks of the Crick Wheare
We Camped for the night fine grass for the Horses—the timber on
the mountains Heare is Pitch Pine Spruce Pine Hemlock and
quakenasp the latter of Which there are vast quantityes. In the bottoms along the Cricks Cotten Wood Black alder and Willows With
the Chock Cherry Black Curren [currant] goosbery and Wild Rose
on the Hill Sides are Some Small White oak Brush from one to
fifteen feet High and I Have Seen Some large Enof for a Handspike
Every thing of the shrub or tree [kinds] that Bair frute is now In full
Blume—the Choack Cherry is on[e] of the Handsomest Bushes I
Have Seen and is now In full Blume—

Satterday 2nd June 1822

Hard frost our Horses much Scattered this morning and it Was late
When We Set out up the left Hand fork of the [Ferdinand] Crick
the Hills Close In on both Sides and at about four miles We arive at
the top of the mountain [200] and Crossing over and down a small drean
[drain] about two miles to an oppen valley about two miles Wide
Which We Crossed nearly [at] Right angles pasing a Small Branch [201]
about the midle of the vally Which Runs north a little West from this
We Went up a small Branch betwen High mountains five miles to
the top of the great mountain In low gap   High Peeks on both
Sides of us We pased Into a large plain a little Roleing With Some
groves of trees—and Crossed Several fine Streems of Watter—and all
tho We are on a mountain—the grass Is tall and to all apperence ther
Has ben Sesnable Rains Heare as the old as Well as young grass is
tall and I think from Every apperence this Plain Wold make a good
settlement for farmers. and tho We are on a High mountain We are
not one third of the Hight of the mountain tops We pased threw this

---

An incident that James then recounts, supposedly taking place at San Domingo
on Saturday evening, June 1, and Sunday, June 2, has no counterpart in Fowler's
journal. James's party and Glenn's reached Taos on June 3. James, *Three Years
among the Indians and Mexicans*, pp. 161–63.]

[199] Ferdinand creek; up this to its forks at foot of Taos Pass.

[200] Thus making the Taos Pass, 8450 feet in altitude, and crossing to the
watershed of the Arkansaw; but still far from being out of the mountains.

[201] Cieneguilla creek, running N. down Moreno valley to join Moreno creek,
from the N., on which is Elizabethtown. The confluence of these two creeks, at
the foot of Little Baldy peak, forms Cimarron creek, a tributary of the Canadian
river. Moreno valley separates the Taos range from the Cimarron range, which
latter Fowler is now crossing.

plain about twelve miles the Watters Run Into grand Pirarie and make part of the Kenadean [Canadian] forke of the arkensaw—after pasing this Plain We Began to desend the mountain Which is now Well Covered With timber that is Pine Spruce and quakenasp Pasing down the mountain We found the Rocks very troblesom amongest Which We See a great many Indean graves.[202] or large Piles of loos [s]tone throne up In Heapes—about dark We got to the fut of the mountain and about one mile farther Camped on a Crick of Bold Runing Watter and find our Selves once more In the grand Pirarie of the arkensaw   Cors this day N 80 East 25 miles[203]—Robert Fowler killed two deer In the mountain

[202] [Thomas James reported the same monuments:

At the end of our two days' journey from Taos we encamped at the foot of the mountain near large piles of stones placed on each side of a ravine or gully. These were in shape like immense walls, from ten to sixty feet in length, about ten wide, and from four to six feet in height. They were the tombs of Camanche Indians, who had been massacred at this place many years before by the Spaniards. An old man in Santa Fe whom I employed about my store, informed me of the circumstances of ths [sic] cold-blooded butchery, in which he as a Spanish soldier took part. It happened when my informant was about twenty years of age, which was a few years previous to our Revolutionary war. According to his account, the Spaniards and Camanches had been at war with each other for many years with various fortune on both sides, when the Spanish authorities determined to offer peace to their enemies. For this purpose they marched with a large army to this place of tombs, and encamped, whence they sent out heralds to the Camanches with an invitation to the whole nation to come in and smoke the pipe of peace and bury the hatchet of war forever. The unsuspecting Indians came in, pursuant to the invitation, and brought their women and children to the number of several thousands. The council was held and a solemn treaty formed which one side hoped and expected would be inviolate forever. They smoked the pipe of peace and of brotherhood. Everything betokened lasting harmony, and for three days an apparently friendly and cordial intercourse took place between the two powers. During this time the Spaniards insidously [sic] bought up all the bows and arrows, and other arms of the Indians, at very high prices, and the third day found these simple children of nature stripped of their arms and entirely defenseless. . . . The Spaniards having surrounded the Indians, fell suddenly, at a concerted signal, upon them and killed all without regard to age or sex. The women and children clung to their protectors, who would not leave them and could not fight, and thus they were all slaughtered together. . . . The countrymen of the slaughtered Indians afterwards erected the stone walls near to which we were now encamped, and which covered a large extent of ground, as tombs and monuments for the dead. (James, *Three Years among the Indians and Mexicans*, pp. 164–66)]

[203] About E., over the Cimarron range, passing by Black Peak, 10,900 feet high, to camp in the plains on a tributary of Cimarron creek, a branch of the Canadian (not to be confounded with that vastly larger stream, the Cimarron

monday 3rd June 1822

Set out Early and at about Seven miles pased the Head of a Small Crick but no Watter there Is no appeerence of Rain Hear for a long time—the ground is as dry as dust the grass not began to Sprout and Every thing look like the dead of Winter—and Still more So When We turn our Eye to the top of the mountain and see the Snow Which Is Still In Sight—at twelve miles We Crosed a bold Streem of Watter [204] 30 feet Wide it Cors South East—and at Eight miles farther We Camped on the bank of deep Crick [205] about 20 feet Wide Runs South—on the low bottoms of this Crick the grass begins to gro a little Heare Is much sign of Bever—Corse North 45 East 20 miles

tusday 4th June 1822

We Set out Early leaveing the mountain on our left tho Some of the Spurs pass in frunt of us and Exstend Some distance to our Right those Spurs We Have to Cross—and the appeer Some distance a Head at twelve miles Stoped for dinner on a branch [206] 20 feet Wide Runs South much Sign of Bever—In the Evening We Went up the Crick Eight miles and Camped [207] Ward killed one Cabery our Corse this [day] North 45 E 18 [sic] miles

Wensday 5th June 1822

We Went up the Crick 10 miles and Stoped for dinner In the afternoon We Went up the Crick 3 miles and Camped at a large Spring the Spanierd tells us that If We go from this We Will Have no Watter to night Robert Fowler killed two deer and Ward one—

---

river, which is a branch of the Arkansaw itself). Cimarron creek, after issuing from the mountains, and having been joined by Ponil creek on one side and Rayado creek on the other, falls into the Canadian river; on it are the towns of Cimarron and Springer, Colfax Co., N. M.

[204] Cimarron creek, as already said.

[205] Vermejo creek, next considerable branch of the Canadian from the W. above Cimarron creek. It falls into the Canadian between stations Dover and Dorsey of the A., T. and S.F.R.R.

[206] The Canadian river itself, which Fowler appears to have struck somewhere about the mouth of Tenaja creek, from the E. This is in the vicinity of Maxwell's station, a noted place in the old days of staging, which I well remember, having arrived there at 5 p. m. of Friday, June 10, 1864.

[207] Position uncertain—see next note.

James & mcnight party kill one deer Heare the men geathered Some Wild Ineons [onions]—

the grass is a little better than Wheare We first Came Into the Pirarie   Cors No 50 East 13 miles[208]

thorsday 6th June 1822

Set out Early up the Spur of the mountain and at about one mile We arived on a High Beed of table land about Eight miles Wide this land[209] is leavel and Rich the grass about nee High and Has all the appeerence of Haveing Had Seasnable Rains   While in the low grounds on both Sides the ground is as dry as dust We pased on this High land one fine Spring of Watter We Seen two Buffelow and Some Caberey—

We Hear for the first time Seen the long Billed Bird[210] it is about the Size of a fesent and the Same Collor the legs and neck about like our Common dung Hill fowls—the Bill about one foot in length and

[208] It is impossible to ascend the Canadian river *any* distance on such a course, as the river is running due S. along here, after coming E. from the mountains. Fowler was camped last night at some uncertain point on the Canadian and on the present railroad line, which runs due N. through Raton pass, across the boundary between New Mexico and Colorado at 37°, and past Fisher's peak to Trinidad, on Purgatory river. But Fowler makes altogether too much easting for any such course as this. I understand, after careful consideration of his meager indications, that his "up the crick" so many miles means up the Canadian to the mouth of Chico Rico creek, a branch from the N. E. which, if followed up, would take him through Manco Burro Pass, between the Raton Mesa and the Chico Rico Mesa, to a tributary of Purgatory river; but that, having gone up Chico Rico creek to the confluence of its Una de Gato branch, he follows up the latter to camp at the foot of the Chico Rico Mesa. In no other way can we follow him "up a crick" continuously in anything like the direction or to anything like the distance he gives; and that this was the way he went will presently appear.

[209] Chico Rico Mesa, a part of the general Raton plateau, separated from Raton Mesa proper by the defile known as Manco Burro Pass.

[210] He means the chaparral cock or road-runner, *Geococcyx californianus*, though he makes its bill about six times too long.

[This curious ground cuckoo is mentioned by many travelers in the southwestern United States. It is also called snake killer and *paisano*. The bird is nearly two feet long, about half its length being its tail. The plumage is bronze or coppery green, changing to a dark steel blue on the head. The bird is noted for its swiftness on the ground, and with the propulsion of both feet and wings it can move as fast as a horse. Apparently it can be domesticated and makes a very satisfactory pet. Gregg, *Commerce of the Prairies*, p. 138.]

about one Inch In deameter at the Head and Smaller at the point—
We Crosed this plind [plain] and down the mountain to a branch of
the White Bair Crick [211] Heare is good Watter and plenty of Wood—
We Stoped for dinner—after Which We move on about 10 miles
farther and Camped on the Same Branch [212] a buffelow Was killed
and braught Into Camp   We now leave the main mountain at a
great distance on our left and the Spur to the Right   Corse N° 20
East fifteen miles [19 by above text].

friday 7th June 1822

Set out Early and Steered for the point of the Spur of the mountain
to our Right—at about 16 miles Stoped for dinner on a Crick
Haveing one Hole of Watter—the Ballence being [dry] for some
distance after dinner We proceded on leaveing the Spur of the
mountain on the Right—and then Steered for a Small mountain
Standing By its Self and leaveing it on our Right fel on the Head of a
Branch that Was dry We Went down that about five miles and
found Watter In the night Some of the party did not Come up till
next morning—

    the Pirarie over Which We pased to day is a little Roleing but So
dry for the Want of Rain that grass is not more than one Inch and
a Half long in any place

[211] That is to say, Purgatory river, at the mouth of which Lewis Dawson was
killed by a grizzly bear: see p. 47, Nov. 13, 1821. Fowler had no name for this
large river, excepting that it was Pike's "1st Fork," and here speaks of it in terms
which recall the tragedy.

[212] Chaquaqua creek, a large branch of Purgatory river, draining N. from
Chico Rico Mesa. Crossing this mesa in the direction said, Fowler passes at 37° the
line between New Mexico and Colorado at the same place that the Denver,
Texas, and Ft. Worth R. R. does now—about long. 103° 53′ W.—and comes
down off the mesa about 5 m. due E. of Watervale, Las Animas Co., Col. He
keeps down the creek some 10 m. and camps on it, about opposite the western-
most point of the Mesa de Maya.

    From this point Fowler makes a break, almost as straight as the crow flies, for
the Arkansaw, which he will strike at Coolidge, Kas. It is a long distance across
country, about N. E., with no exactly identifiable landmark till we stand him on
Two Buttes; and his trail does not coincide, except approximately, with any road
I can find laid down on the best modern maps. The nearest I know of is what is
called the "probable course" of the wagon road from Cimarron to Granada,
on the drainage sheet of Hayden's Atlas of Colorado, 1877; but the maps I go
by are the later ones of the U. S. Geological Survey, 2 m. to the inch. It is a matter
of special interest to recover this old trail as closely as possible.

Cors this day north 55 East 30 miles five miles Was in the night—[213]

Satterday 8th June 1822

We did not Set out till late Waiting for the three men that lay out— the arived about Eight oclock We then Set out and maid twenty miles—and Camped at a Small Hole of Watter that you Cold Smell 50 yds When Stired—for all the anemels for many miles Round Come there to drink—We Have no Wood and Burn the Buffelow dung to Cook We are now In the oppen World not a tree Bush or Hill of any kind to be Seen for When you take the Eye of [off] the ground you See nothing but the Blue Horeson Cors this day north 60 East 17 [sic] miles [214] Ward and McKnight killed one Buffelow Bull—

Sunday 9th June 1822

Set out Early over the leavel Smoth Pirarie   We Soon See a mound a Head in the Pirarie for Which We Steered it bore north 30 East— We Crossed Several Watter Corses all makeing South East but all dry We Stoped for dinner at a Small mud Hole Whear We maid fire of the Buffelow dung and cooked our dinner We then moved on and Camped on a Crick [215] of of Clear Watter Whear there Was Wood

[213] A long lap in the open to a blind camp, and copy a little vitiated by some interlineation not quite clear. But we can follow the trail pretty closely. The "mountain to our right" is the general elevation of the Mesa de Maya, along which Fowler passes about E. N. E., crossing successive dry drains of tributaries of Purgatory river, all running to his left. Rounding the extreme W. point of the Mesa said, Fowler steers past "a small mountain standing by itself," which appears to be, by a singular coincidence, an isolated part of the general elevation now known as *Fowler* Mesa. Further on E. along the N. border of the Maya Mesa, is the better-known Mt. Carrizo, capped by Potatoe Butte; the line between Las Animas and Baca counties cuts this isolated elevation about lat. 37° 10′ N., and long. 103° 05′ W. Camp cannot be far from the obscure place called Willow Spring, on one of the collateral sources of Two Butte creek—possibly at that identical water-hole.

[Fowler is now on the route followed by Pedro de Villasur in 1720 on his disastrous expedition to the Great Plains.]

[214] Passing from Las Animas Co. to camp at some indeterminable point in Baca Co., west of Springfield. From the degree of easting made, and what is presently said of the S. E. course of the dry washes to be passed to-morrow, I suppose Fowler to be among the numberless and nameless drains which make for tributaries of Cimarron river.

[215] Two Butte creek, at a point Fowler gives as 3 m. short of the Two Buttes whence it takes its name. Camp is still in Baca Co., but very near the border of Prowers Co. Fowler's "mound" above said is Two Buttes, a conspicuous

and good grass for the Horses—the Buffelow killed this day Was two
Poor for use and not Buchered the grass is Heare Better and there is
sign of there Haveing been Some Rain Heare lately—
   Cors north 30 East 25 miles

monday 10th June 1822

Set out Early and at three miles pased the mound[216] it Stands on
the north Side of the Crick and about two miles from it I Went to the
top of it Which Has two Heads about 70 yds apart Standing north
and South of Each other and is about two Hundred feet High and
about 300 threw the Baces the tops or Heads Consist mostly of
Rocks Pilled By nature on Each other   But Has been Some What
Improved by the Indeans to make it aplace of defence as Well as
place of look out—the Spanish name of the mound tewenna—from
Heare We See another Branch[217] on our left and a Cross the main
Crick another to the South all makeing a north East Corse—We
Continu on twelve miles and Stoped for dinner on the left Hand
forke and at Eight miles further Camped[218] on the main Crick a
little above the forkes the Chanel is Heare about 60 yds Wide and
We Have to dig Holes In the Sand to get Watter there being none
above ground—Eaight Buffelow Was killed this day—our Corse
N° 55 East 20 miles

tusday 11th June 1822

Set out Early Crosing the Crick and leaveing it on our left Hand
Steered north 55 East at fifteen miles We See the valley of the
arkensaw and on looking [back] We Can See the mound in full vew—
at twenty miles stoped for diner on the arkensaw[219]—at an Island

---

landmark, the first absolutely identifiable one we have had for several days. The
principal one of his several dry water-courses is Bear creek, that tributary of the
Cimarron which runs past Springfield.

[216] Two Buttes, position as said with reference to Two Butte creek, and 1 m.
due N. of the boundary between Baca and Prowers counties.

[217] North Butte creek, principal fork of Two Butte creek.

[218] On Two Butte creek, a little above the confluence of North Butte creek,
having passed from Baca Co. into Prowers Co. when opposite the Two Buttes.
If he had kept on a little further, about 4 m. below the forks, he would have
reached Butte Springs, and need not have dug for water.

[219] Striking the Arkansaw about opposite Coolidge, in Kansas near the border
of Colorado. Camp of Nov. 4, 1821, which Fowler presently mentions, was a
mile lower down. As he says on Nov. 5 that he went 9 m. to reach "a large

Covered With timber and some trees on the South Side of the River there Is Sevral Islands Heare Some Covered With Willow about one mile below the Island there is an old large Cotten Wood tree Stands on a point of High land—Cheefly Composed of gravel our Corse north 55 East 20 miles

11th June [continued.]

after dinner We proceded down the River ten miles and Camped[220] on the Bank In a grove of trees opeset an Island—the Sand Hills lay South of Camp With Some Cotten Wood trees on them—We pased the Camp Wheare We Slept on the fourth of november [1821] about one mile below Wheare We Struck the River to day—

Wensday 12th June 1822

We Set out at the ushal time down the River and pasing the Camp at the Bever Sign Where We lay on the 3rd of november last Continu to the Point of Rocks and Hoop Wood trees—Wheare a party of Indeans appeered on Hors back on the opeset Side of the River— We Hailed them the answered but Wold not Come a Cross—We then Camped for the night—the Indeans moved off and Soon after a party of White men appeered on the Same Side one of them Came over to our Camp this Was Conl Cooppers party[221] from Boons lick

crick" (Two Butte creek), he appears to have struck the Arkansaw 8 m. below that creek—*i. e.*, about opposite Coolidge, as just said.

[Here the party turned downstream along the Arkansas River, following the route that would become the Santa Fe Trail.]

[220] Vicinity of Syracuse, Hamilton Co., Kas.

[221] No doubt Braxton Cooper, from Daniel Boone's salt works, which were about 4 m. from Franklin, Mo. See Lewis and Clark, ed. of 1893, p. 18, and Pike, ed. of 1895, pp. 367, 570.

[The "Conl Coopper" to whom Fowler refers was Colonel Benjamin Cooper, leader of the party. It included in its membership of twelve or thirteen his two nephews Braxton and Stephen Cooper. The salt spring to which Coues refers was discovered before the Louisiana Purchase by French trappers and hunters. It got its name, Boone's Lick, from the fact that Nathan and Daniel M. Boone, sons of the Kentucky pioneer, made salt there in the summer of 1807. Kate L. Gregg, "History of Fort Osage," *Missouri Historical Review*, XXXIV (July 1940), 467; and Gregg, *Commerce of the Prairies*, p. 14 n.

Thomas James confirms the encounter with the Cooper party from Boone's Lick and continues with a series of incidents, supposedly taking place from this time through June 19, which are intended to be highly discreditable to Glenn. James, *Three Years among the Indians and Mexicans*, pp. 167–74.]

on their Way to the Spanish Settlement With Some goods and Some traps to take Bever

thorsday 13th June 1822

Set out Early pasing the french Camp at five miles and Stoped for dinner at the Island Wheare We lodged on the 30th of october last then moved down the River about ten miles Camped on an Island makeing 30 miles—

Friday 14th June 1822

moved on Early and Pased our Camp of the 29th octobr last—and all So pased the Camp of the 28th and Camped opeset to an Island Wheare We Sent the Horses for the night—this day James and party left us and Commenced Crossing the River about 12 oclock takeing three of our Party With them—that Was duglas Priar and [illegible 222] —maid 25 miles

Satterday 15th June 1822

moved at Sun Rise down the River fifteen miles and Comenced Crossing for Which purpose We used the green Hide of a buffelow Bull by Way of a boat 223—Heare are Some thousands of Buffelow to be Seen at one vew—I beleve We Have not been out of Sight of Buffelow Since We Came to the River Except in the night and When darke So that the Hunters Have Killed When the plased—We got on the north Side of the River and While We Ware Sadling up the Horses James and party pased us. it may be Remarked Heare that

222 George Douglas, Nathaniel Pryor, and one unidentifiable man. The blind word looks like "Rohland" or "Soulard," but is nothing like any name previously occurring in this MS. It must be that of some man who joined the party at Taos, or else the missing Christian name of one of the party mustered in note 12.

[John Rowland (1791–1873) was born in Maryland; little is known of his early years. Hitherto it has been supposed that he came to New Mexico in 1823. Later "John Roland," a naturalized citizen of Mexico, farmer, and distiller, was reported by Charles Bent as one of twenty-two Americans living in Taos in 1841. David J. Weber, "John Rowland," in Hafen, *Mountain Men and the Fur Trade of the Far West*, IV, 275–81; Sister Mary Loyola, "The American Occupation of New Mexico, 1821–1852," *New Mexico Historical Review*, XIV (January 1939), 67; and Joseph J. Hill, "Ewing Young in the Fur Trade of the Far Southwest, 1822–1834," *Oregon Historical Quarterly*, XXIV (March 1923), 9. See also Carter, *Territorial Papers*, XV, 696 n, 711, 732.]

223 [A bull-boat, which the Plains Indians made when conditions were favorable, was constructed by stretching a green buffalo hide over a willow framework. The craft resembled a tub and was capable of carrying a considerable weight.]

the River Was little more than Belly deep to the Horses. But for feer of the quick Sand it Was thaught best take all the Bagage over In the Boat and Send the Horses over Enty [empty] Waiding the River our Selves and drag the boat Wheare the Watter at times Was not more than Six Inches deep—as Soon as We Ware Readey We moved on Six miles pasing findleys Island [224] and Camped about Half a mile below James and party—

Sunday 16th June 1822

James and Party pased us Early down the River We Steered a little north of East to Cut off a bend of the River [225] makeing 25 miles and lay In Sight of the timber on the River large droves of Buffelow all day In Sight duglas and Prior Join us to day

monday 17th June 1822

moved on Early maid 25 miles and camped on the West Side of Buffelow [Coon] Creek at the Same place Wheare We Camped on the We Camped on the 21st of octobr last—James and Party Camp Close to us—Heare We Sopose We Cold See at one time ten thousand Buffelow

tusday 18th June 1822

We Comenced Crosing the Crick Early it being about mid Side deep to the Horses and the Banks Steep and mudey the men Waided and Carryed over all the Packs and then led or drove the Horses a Cross— We then moved on about Eight miles and meet With Some Pawne Indeans—With Home [whom] We Camped—there Was With them one of the Ietan Cheefs Who Stated that He Was lately from Was[h]ington Cetey—In the Corse of the Evening the Indeans Collected to the nomber of from four to five Hunderd [226]—it is Hear proper to mention that Capt James Had two Spanierds With Him and that Conl glann Head two all So—but the last two Ware dresed like our Selves—but James Spanierds Wore their own Clothing and Ware Challenged by the Indeans as their Enemeys—a Councel Was

[224] Unidentified—named for one of the party. See back, Oct. 22, p. 36.

[225] Hitherto Fowler has retraced his steps down the Arkansaw, and the points passed are easily reckoned by back references. But here he leaves the river to cut off the large bend it makes in sweeping past Ford, where Mulberry creek comes in. For this "dry route" see Pike, ed. of 1895, pp. 433, 434.

[226] [Thomas James told the story that follows in quite a different way. James, *Three Years among the Indians and Mexicans*, pp. 168–72.]

Held Which lasted about two Hours the Inquirey Was Whether these men Ware Spanierds if so the must be killed as Ietan Cheef Insisted the Ware Spanierds and must be killed but the Pawne Cheef Refused to Have them killed till He new the Ware Spanierds the two men Ware Sot In the midle of the Councel and there Interageted but maid no answer leting on that the did not no What Was Said to them—to Which the had ben advised before they Ware takeing In to the Councel most of those Indeans understand the Spanish language but Cold not git one Word from the men the then asked Mr Roy the Inturpurter If those men Ware not Spanierds He told the Indeans He did not kno Who the Ware that He Cold not Speeke their langage to Which the Ietan Cheef Replyed you do not kno thim you kno How to gave them Horses and Can tell them How to Ride and yet you Can not Spapke to them Which is a little Strange How do you git them to Eat or Whare did you git them We See them Ride on your Horses—to Which mr Roy answers as followes— for it is Hear now be Com nesceery to fib a little—that about two days back We met a party of White men going up the River and that those men Ware With them that the Ware from St lewis and Wanted to go back and Had Come this far With us that We Head Some Spare Horses and that the Had got on and Road—the Pawne Cheef then Said that Some four or five years back He Had Seen Some English men and french men together and the Cold not talk to Each other that maybe those Ware English men—to Which Mr Roy answered that He Cold not talk English and did not kno these men—and So the Councel Ended the two Spanierds Pased for English men tho the Ware nearly as Black as pall—but at all Events the Ware Blacker than the Indeans them Selves—

We are now on the Crick noted on the 20th of october last [Pawnee fork.]—We Remained Heare all night but In the Evening the Indeans [s]tole all the neck Roaps of our Horses—We then took the lash Roaps and tyed up the Horses the Pawne Cheef Slept In our Camp— and after Some presents of knives from Conl glann and Hors from Capt James We Head lev to proced as Soon as We pleased In the morning—

Wensday 19th June 1822

We Set out Early the Indeans appeer frendly—We moved on about five miles and looking behind We See the Indeans Runing after us— and all tho We drove the Horses In a trot the Will overtake us In a few minets—We Conclude it best to Stop and let them Come up

Which Was done—We Stood prepaired for Battle But Will Receve them frendly if We Can—now the Inturpreter prepaired a pipe and offered them a Smoke as the Came up Which the all axcepted of and looking amongest [us] asked Wheare the two men Ware Which the Soposed to be Spanierds and Ware Shone them—the then Went and Shook Hands With us all pointed us the Road Which We took and the Indeans Went Back the Ware fourteen In nomber—We then pushed on to the Pawne River [227] Wheare Crossed and Stoped for dinner Heare is large Hords of Buffelow one Cow Was Killed and braught In to Camp—We moved on In the afternoon and Went nineteen miles makeing 39 miles and Camped [228] on the River Bank the[n] We traveled Some time In the night for feer the Indeans Will follow and steel our Horses—James and His party did not Come up—

thorsday 20th June 1822

We Set out Early and Steered north 60 East Intending to go Close to the South Side of the Sand Hills as We Cannot travel threw them We Ware detained about two Hours By a Storm of Hail and Rain after Which We Went to a Crick [229] Wheare We found Some drift Wood and Camped for the night makeing 20 miles N° 60 East James and party Bore off to the Right down the River—

Friday 21st June 1822

Sot out late Some of our Horses Had gon a great distance from Camp—We Pased Close to the Sand Hills pasing several fine Springs Runing out of them to the South   and In the Evening Camped on

[227] Of our author = Walnut creek, near Great Bend: see back, note 48.

[228] Vicinity of Raymond, Rice Co.

[229] Cow creek or one of its branches; vicinity of Lyons, seat of Rice Co.

Fowler has left the Arkansaw and taken up a devious 'cross country route, which is to bring him through Kansas into Missouri near Kansas City and so on through Independence, Mo., to Fort Osage, on the Missouri river. In 1822 the road which soon became the long famous Santa Fé caravan route from Independence to the great bend of the Arkansaw was hardly established. This went through Council Grove, by the most direct way which the traders found it convenient to take. For an examination of this route see Pike, ed. of 1895, pp. 517–522. It is interesting to note, as showing that no such route as this had become established and well known when Fowler went through, that he deviates widely from what would have been his most direct and in every way most eligible line of march. As we recover his trail we shall find it to be one now unknown, looping far to the S. into Butler Co., then passing heads of the Verdigris, crossing the Neosho below the mouth of the Cottonwood, and so on eastward with the requisite northing. I regard the trail we now take up as something of an unexpected discovery.

the little arkensaw—We Seen James and partey this day at a great distance to our Right makeing down the [Arkansaw] River the Cuntry threw Which We pased this day is leavel and Rich the grass tall and Has all the appeerence of Seasnable Rains. We Have In our openion layed down the Pawne River [=Walnut cr.] as the line betwen the Wet and dry Weather or the long and Short grass— maid 30 miles north [*read* south] 60 East [230]

Satterday 22nd June 1822

We Set out Early Crossing Several Branches [231] all Running to the Right We Camped on a Branch of White River [232] about 20 feet Wide With High Banks—the Pirarie this day is leavel and Rich the land Black mixed With lime Stone—the grass So tall that In [it] is Hard on the Horses to Brake it down—no more Buffelow to be Seen I beleve We Have left them all be Hind and Will be Hard Run for meat— maid 20 miles South 65 East

230 From any position in which last night's camp can have been, it is impossible to bring Fowler to the Little Arkansaw on any such course as *N.* 60° E. 30 miles. That course and distance would take him far beyond the Little Arkansaw, to some point about the heads of Turkey cr., N. of McPherson. Moreover, he would never have seen the other party making down the Arkansaw. Once more, the change I have made in reading the text is required by what follows. He can be brought in "30" miles *S.* 60° E. to the Little Arkansaw somewhere about the mouth of Turkey creek, in Harvey Co. Observe that to-morrow's course, S. 65° E., is practically in the same direction he travels to-day.

[In April 1843, Don Antonio José Chavez, on his way from Santa Fe to Missouri with two wagons, five servants, fifty-five mules, and $10,000 or $12,000 in specie or gold bullion, was waylaid on the Little Arkansas here, robbed, and murdered. The deed was committed by a band of fifteen cutthroats under one John McDaniel. The lawless band was hunted down, and ten of them, including the leader, were captured and tried in the United States federal court at St. Louis. McDaniel and his brother were convicted of murder and executed. The others were sentenced to fine and imprisonment. Gregg, *Commerce of the Prairies*, pp. 337–38. See note 40 above.]

231 Of the Little Arkansaw, running S.; these are the Emma creeks and Sand creek, the latter flowing through Newton, Harvey Co.

232 Walnut creek—not to be confounded with the other of the same name which joins the Arkansaw near Great Bend. This Walnut creek falls into the Arkansaw near the border of Oklahoma, being the one called White river by Fowler on Oct. 9 (p. 27), one of whose branches is still known as Whitewater. Camp is on one of these, near the boundary between Harvey and Butler counties. We now realize what a roundabout route Fowler is taking from the great bend of the Arkansaw to Fort Osage on the Missouri, being far S. of the regular "Santa Fé Trail" that was soon to become established.

Sunday 23rd June 1822

Rained Hard last night—

We Sot out about 9 oclock Crosing three Branches [233] Runing to the South all Well timbered Rich lime Stone land a little Roleing. We Camped on the third Branch—no game—

Maid 20 miles N° 80 East

Rained all night—

monday 24 June 1822

We Sot out Early and it Soon began to Rain   We maid Six miles Crossing two Branches [234] and Camped on the Second Which is Well timbered With Walnut Buckiey Hickory oak and Elm. the land of the Richest kind—lime Stone In all Banks but the leave [level] land Clar of Stone—

6 miles north 65 East

Rained all night

tusday 25th June 1822

Set out about 10 oclock up the Branch and out at the Head of it and over a low deviding Ridge and fell on the Head Watters of the virdegree. [235] the land is more Roleing the Hills Higher but Rich We Camped on a Branch Runing nearly West With Some timber Peno killed one deer

maid 15 miles no 50 East

Wensday 26th June 1822

We Sot out Early pasing over a Rich Roleing Pirarie to a Crick [236] With Some timber—taylor killed two deer—We maid 8 miles no 15 East   It Rains Heavely—

[233] Of the same Walnut creek, on a course nearly E., in Butler Co.

[234] Of the same Walnut creek—the second branch above said being the main source of this stream, interlocking with a source of the south fork of Cottonwood river, nearly on the line between Butler and Chase counties. Camp about the place called Sycamore Springs, in Butler Co.

[235] Not quite yet—Fowler has still to pass the heads of the south fork of the Cottonwood, which he mistakes for those of the Verdigris. No head of the Verdigris flows anything like west, as he says that branch does on which he camps. All his indications set camp unmistakably at or near Thurman, Chase Co., on that branch of Thurman creek which runs westerly. This creek is joined at Matfield Green by two others, the three together composing the south fork of the Cottonwood, running N. This is a queer place to find a man on his way from Great Bend to Kansas City—but here he is!

[236] Head of Verdigris river, in Chase Co., at the distance and in the direction said from Thurman.

thorsday 27th June 1822

Set out Early Crossing five Cricks[237] all Runing South East Some timber on all of them one twenty yds Wide the Cuntry as ushal Rich and Roleing—Robert Fowler and Ward Each killed one deer— maid 15 miles N 25 East

Friday 28th June 1822

Set out Early Crossing a Crick at Six miles Runing South and at 12 miles Cam to grand River or the Six Bull [the Neosho,[238] running] South East   Went up it about one mile Crossed over and Camped on a Crick near the mouth this Crick Puts In on the north Side Heare Is one of the Best trakes [tracts] of land for a settlement I Have Seen the land is Rich and leavel Plenty of timber on the Crick as Well as all a long the River—taylor killed one Elk—Which Was Braught to Camp We maid 12 miles no 40 East

Satterday 29th June 1822

Set out Early and at ten miles Crosed a Crick[239] 50 yds Wide part of

[237] The Verdigris itself and four of its collateral heads, named Camp, Fawn, Rock, and Moon. Fowler's trail here crosses that of Pike, who was camped on one of these creeks Sept. 10, 1806. For the remarkable fan-shaped leash of streamlets which compose the headwaters of the Verdigris, see Pike, ed. of 1895, p. 400. Camp in vicinity of Olpe, Lyon Co. ·

[238] The Neosho is struck at a point between Neosho Rapids and the mouth of the Cottonwood, some 8 m. a little S. of E. from Emporia, seat of Lyon Co.

[This crossing was made about thirty miles below Council Grove. George C. Sibley, Benjamin Reeves, and Thomas Mather, commissioners appointed to survey and mark the road to Santa Fe, named the place Council Grove, and there they met fifty of the principal chiefs and warriors of the Great and Little Osages on August 10, 1825, to conclude the treaty that guaranteed free passage over the road from the Missouri River to the Mexican boundary. The three requisites for Plains travel—wood, water, and grass—were plentiful, and here was found the last source of hard wood to be taken down the trail to repair wagons. Within a few years the place thus became the rendezvous for the annual traders' caravans bound for Santa Fe. The area became part of the Kaw Indian reservation in 1846. In 1847, Seth M. Hays, the first white settler, opened his "Last Chance" store. The Methodist church established a mission here in 1850. Gregg, *The Road to Santa Fe*, pp. 33–34; Thomas F. Doran, "Kansas Sixty Years Ago," *Kansas Historical Collections*, XV (1919–22), 483; and Gregg, *Commerce of the Prairies*, pp. 29–30.]

[239] Marais des Cygnes creek, continuation of Marais des Cygnes river, as the main course of the Osage river in Kansas is still called, by curious survival of the pure French phrase. This stream is struck in the vicinity of Reading, Lyon Co.,

the Racuon fork of the osage River [240] the Corse South East—at 14 miles Crosed a Branch of the Same Crick—and at 22 miles Camped Without Wood—Had no fier—the first 10 miles N 15 E the last 12 miles N 65 E the Bottoms Has Some timber the land all Rich Rained Heavily all night With thonder and lightning—

22 miles the first 10 N 15 E then 12 N 65 E

Sunday 30th June 1822

last night's Rain Wett all our Bagage as Well as the bever furr the morning Clear We dry all our things and move on about 10 oclock—at 10 miles Crossed a Crick [241] and at Sixteen miles Crosed the osage River [242] Wheare We left one Hors He Coud not Rais up the Bank Which Was High and mudey—We moved out of the timber and Slept on a High point to avoid the the musketoes Ward killed one young Elk We Have Seen many Elk In the two last days Rained Heavily all night

maid 16 miles N 65 E

monday 1st July 1822

the last night Raised the Cricks So that We Have to leave the Waggon [road] We fell into two days back Which Road Was maid by Becknal and His party on their Way to the Spanish Settlement—We

---

nearly on the border of Osage Co.; whence Fowler proceeds about E. N. E. across Cherry creek, to camp on the divide between Marais des Cygnes creek and its Salt creek branch—somewhere between Olivet and Osage City, seat of Osage Co.

[Lyndon is the seat of Osage County.]

240 [William Becknell, with twenty-one men and three wagons, passed this way during the first half of June 1822 on his second trip to Santa Fe. He encountered serious difficulty with Osage Indians but was rescued by Colonel A. P. Chouteau; then he crossed the Arkansas River at the Caches, reached his destination, and returned home in the fall. William Becknell, "Journal of Two Expeditions from Boone's Lick to Santa Fé," pp. 56–68; and James, *Three Years among the Indians and Mexicans*, p. 175 n.]

241 Salt creek, crossed in the vicinity of Lyndon, seat of Osage Co.

242 Dragoon creek of present nomenclature, considered by Fowler as the main Osage river. It is a large stream, about the size of the Marais des Cygnes itself, separated from the latter by Salt creek—all three of these coming together within a mile or two of each other, in the immediate vicinity of Quenemo, Osage Co., close to the border of Franklin Co. For Dragoon cr., see Pike, ed. of 1895, p. 520. Fowler is now nearing what was soon to become the regular Santa Fé caravan route from Independence, Mo., to the great bend of the Arkansaw—after having needlessly made a great bend of his own southward from that direct line of travel.

Hear took up a low Ridge betwen the Branches and over a low Ridge Eight miles to a large Crick [243] So Raised With the last night Rain that the loads on the Horses Will git Wett If We drive them threw But the men Waid over and Carry the Pack on their Heads—the Watter Swims the Horses—Heare is a large Bodey of timber along this Crick and land of the Best qualety for the Hole Cuntry is fit for Cultevation We Went Six miles In the Evening Crossing two Crick [244] all the Watters Runs South East maid 14 miles N 20 E the timber Increses as We aproch the mesurey [Missouri]

tusday 2nd July 1822

a Heavey thonder Storm Came on in the night and Rained Hard till Sun Rise We then Sot out and Crosing Several Small Branches [245] much Raised With last nights Rain maid five miles and Stoped to dry

[243] Appanoose creek, a branch of the Marais des Cygnes which falls in near Ottawa, seat of Franklin Co., into which Fowler has passed from Osage Co.

"In 1812 a Captain Becknell, who had been on a trading expedition to the country of the Comanches in the summer of 1811, and had done remarkably well, determined the next season to change his objective point to Santa Fé," says Inman, p. 38. When at or near the Caches on the Arkansaw, he left that stream and took his party across country on the Cimarron or dry route; but they were obliged to return, after suffering horribly from thirst, and follow up the Arkansaw route to Taos.

"The virtual commencement of the Santa Fé trade dates from 1822"; and in 1824 was made the first attempt to introduce wagons, etc., says Inman, p. 51. According to Gregg, a better authority, both pack animals and wagons were used 1822–25, but after that wagons only. According to Fowler's passage above, we see that Becknell had taken wagons in 1822 if not earlier; and thus the party to which Col. Marmaduke was attached, and which reached Santa Fé with wagons in 1824, was not the first to pass through Kansas on wheels.

[Inman appears to have confused the dates of the two Becknell expeditions. Coues sensed the error and was correct in preferring the authority of Josiah Gregg. The first recorded use of wagons on the Santa Fe Trail was that of Becknell on his second expedition in the summer of 1822. Gregg, *Commerce of the Prairies*, p. 16 n.]

[244] One of these is Eight Mile creek, next branch of the Marais des Cygnes, falling in near the mouth of the Appanoose, at Ottawa. As "all the Watters runs South East," we know that Fowler is still on the Osage watershed, and I am inclined to set his camp on one of the heads of Ottawa creek, some 6 m. W. of Baldwin City, Douglas Co., perhaps not far from Willow Springs camp of the raders; for which see Pike, ed. of 1895, p. 519.

[245] Heads of the Ottawa creek last said, especially of its East fork. Fowler passes Baldwin City to camp on the divide between the Osage and the Kansan waters.

our Bagage—Heare Some Hunters Sot out to kitt meet [kill meat] Robert Fowler and Taylor Set out In frunt to meet at the Crick a Head of Which We Cold See the timber—We Sot out In the Evening —the gide Chaing His Corse did not meet the Hunters We maid 12 miles and Slept on the devideing Ridge [246] betwen the oasage [Osage] and Kensa or Caw [Kansas] Rivers—the Hunters did not Come In—We See on our left Hand a large Bodey of timber Soposed to be on the Caw River the Pirarie is a little Roleing and of the Richest kind of lime Stone land   We maid 17 miles N 75 East

thorsday [Wednesday] 3rd July 1822

We Sot out Early and like a Ship With out a Rudder We Steerd from South East to north East—I Sopose the gide Was lost or did not as He Had toled us kno Wheare He Was—In this [way] We maid twelve miles and Stoped for noon for We Have not much to Eat tho We See many deer and Some Elk—the two Hunters not Come up yet—We moved on In the Evening and Soon fell on the Waggon Road We had left at the osage River this We followed ten miles and Camped on a Crick [247] Runing north West—and We Sopose to the Caw River—Ward killed a fatt Elk this Evening   the Hunters not up—

We maid 22 miles N 30 East

Rich leavel land—

thorsday 4th July 1822

We Set out Early to follow the Waggon Road but Heare the Pirarie Has Been Burned In the Spring and the grass So gron up So that We Cannot find it—and after Winding about for about two Hours Steered N 45 East Six miles and fell on a Road Runing nearly East and West—along Which We took [to] the East Eand Wheare We found the Waggon tracks—a large Bodey of timber on our left and

[246] Position not exactly determinable, somewhere between Baldwin City and Edgerton, in the vicinity of Black Jack: see Pike, ed. of 1895, p. 519. The divide is here between heads of Big Bull creek, tributary to the Osage, on the S., and heads of Captain creek, a branch of Kansas river, on the N.—Captain creek being the first branch from the S. below the mouth of Wakarusa creek, which latter falls into the Kansas at Eudora. From present camp Fowler passes into the watershed of the Kansas river.

[247] Cedar creek, a branch of Kansas river, as Fowler supposed. Camp on it in the vicinity of Olathe, Johnson Co., Kas. See Pike, ed. of 1895, p. 510. The direct distance is much less than "22" m.; but the party wandered about all the morning.

is Shorly the mesurey or the Caw River and at about Six miles Stoped for dinner—While Heare the lost men Came up the Ware much Woren down there feet Sore and mogersons Woren out—We Went ten miles In the Evening along the Road Crossing one Crick[248] Which Runs north—

the large Bodey of timber Still Continus on our left
the general Corse of this Road is north Eighty East—

Friday 5th July 1822

Sot out Early and at five miles Crossing a large Crick[249] 50 yds Wide Runs north the Bottoms and Hill Sides are Well Covered With timber—We Heare Went up a High Steep Hill over Some Rocks and Continu over High Roleing ground partly Covered With timber and Brush for about four miles then six miles over Roling Pirarie to a Crick[250] Wheare We Stoped for dinner there Is plenty of timber Heare and the gide tells us that He now knos Wheare We are and that it is about ten miles to fort osage We Sot out In the Evening and at three miles Came to a deep Crick[251] Wheare the men Had to Carry the Bagage all over on their Heads and drove the Horses threw—the Watter Was So deep that it Was over the mens Sholders and none but the tall ones Cold Carry the Packs—We then Set out for the fort[252] Wheare We arived about ten oClock at night but our

[248] Turkey creek or a branch of it; this falls into the Kansas river within present limits of Kansas City, Mo. Camp on or near the Kansas-Missouri line, 5 m. from where the road then crossed Big Blue river.

[249] Big Blue river, falling into the Missouri between Kansas City and Independence, Jackson Co., Mo. See Lewis and Clark, ed. of 1893, p. 32, and Pike, ed. of 1895, p. 519. Fowler has just passed from "the Indian Territory" into "the States"—that is, from Kansas into Missouri.

[250] One of several between Big and Little Blue rivers, at or near Independence, Mo.

[251] Little Blue river, the Hay Cabin creek of Lewis and Clark. See ed. of 1893, p. 31.

[The party is now near the site of Independence, Missouri, which was laid out and designated as the county seat of Jackson County in 1827.]

[252] At Fort point, later called Sibley, on the Missouri, between Independence and Lexington, Mo. Fort Osage was built in Sept., 1808, was sometimes called Fort Clark, and in Fowler's time was still an extreme frontier establishment. See Lewis and Clark, ed. of 1893, p. 30.

[In 1808, General William Clark was directed to build a fort on the south side of the Missouri River to serve the dual capacity of military post and trading house for the Osage, Kansas, and Iowa Indians. On August 7 of that year Captain Eli Clemson and his company of eighty-one men, with four keelboats

Company Was much Scattered Haveing Sent mr Roy and Battes forward from the Crick to prepair Supper at the fort fore the Party— on our arivel We Called for them but the Ware not to be found nor Cold We find any purson for Some time but a negro man—and thonder gust Comeing—He Shewed [us] In to mr Sibleys[253] Porch Wheare We Spent the Ballence of the night—

Satterday 6th July 1822

Early In the morning We found mr Boggs[254] the asistant Factor Who Shewed us Into an Enty [empty] House In the garison—to Which We moved our Bagage. Exspecting to Remain there till Some provetions Cold be Precured—

---

loaded with $20,000 worth of trade goods, one with sutlers' goods for the garrison, and another with commissary supplies, embarked at Fort Bellefontaine to establish the new fort 240 miles upstream on the Missouri River. Another party, under General Clark himself, accompanied by eighty St. Charles Dragoons, with Nathan Boone as guide, marched overland for the same place. The spot where they decided to build the fort was on a point overlooking a big eddy in the river. By November 10, 1808, the structure was sufficiently complete for holding a celebration and giving it a name. At this time Fort Osage was the westernmost military outpost of the United States. It was closed in 1827. Gregg, "History of Fort Osage," pp. 439–88.]

[253] [George Champlain Sibley was born in Great Barrington, Massachusetts, on April 1, 1782. In 1800 he became editor of the *Fayetteville* (North Carolina) *Gazette*, and in 1805 he entered government service as an assistant factor in the Indian trading post at Bellefontaine, on the Mississippi River near St. Louis. When Fort Osage was built he became the chief factor there. In 1825 he was appointed as one of the commissioners to survey and map the Santa Fe Trail, and he made a resurvey in 1827. He and his wife, Mary Easton, founded Lindenwood College in St. Charles, Missouri. Gregg, "History of Fort Osage," pp. 440–79.]

[254] [Lilburn W. Boggs was born in Lexington, Kentucky, on December 14, 1792. About 1810 he went to St. Louis, where seven years later he became cashier in the Missouri Bank, the second oldest bank in the city. He married Julia Ann Bent, sister of William and Charles Bent and daughter of Judge Silas Bent. After her death he married Panthea Grant Boone, a granddaughter of Daniel Boone. He was appointed assistant factor at Fort Osage. When the fort was closed he entered mercantile business in towns along the Missouri River and eventually settled in Independence, Missouri, where he engaged in the Santa Fe trade and in trading with the Indians. He was elected lieutenant governor of Missouri in 1832, and governor in 1836. Ten years later he emigrated to California, where he became alcalde of the Northern District. He died on March 4, 1860, on his farm in Napa Valley. William M. Boggs, "A Short Biographical Sketch of Lilburn W. Boggs," *Missouri Historical Review*, IV (January 1910), 106–10.]

the garreson at this time Was Commanded by one officer of the
united States armey—Haveing two men under His Command Both
of them Haveing disarted a few days ago and Carryed off all His
amenetion—now It appeers that mr Boggs Had not advised Him of
our Removel Into the garreson nor did We Sopose from the Shat-
tered Setuation of Every thing We See—that any Command of men
or officer Was there But Whin He looked up In the morning and
Seeing our men and Bagage He Said to mr Boggs that He did not
like to See the gareson taken In that kind of Stile—but on Receeving
that Information from mr Boggs and the officer not Calling on us
We that [thought] Proper not to be longer In His Way and moved
about two Hunderd yds to a Spring and Camped   Wheare after
Some Diffequalty We Precured Some Previtions

It may Heare Be Remarked that. We Ware treeted Heare With
more Coolness than amongest any Indeans or Spanierds We meet
With But We feel greatful to mr Boggs for His Polightness—He in
the morning Precure for us a Small Beef—and mr Sibley Sent us
Some flour and Bacon—Which With Corn meel and Bacon We
Purchased from one of the Citisons We maid out Prete Well—for
two days to Rest and Purchased two Conus [canoes] With a platform
and Shiped all our Baggage With our Selves leaveing four men to
Bring on the Enty Horses to Cortsand Ca [?]—and We proceded to
St lewis 255—Wheare I Remained two days and then took a pasage
In the Steem Boat Calhoon to lewisvill and from that In a Small
Steem Boat to Cincinati—and got Home 256 on the 27th day of July
1822—haveing [been] gon thirteen months and thirteen days

255 [Glenn assigned four men to stay at Fort Osage with the horses and bring
them on by road. He and the rest of his party left the fort on July 9. Their trip
down the Missouri and the Mississippi to St. Louis took five or six days. They
were among American settlements almost all the way; and wherever they stopped
the men probably spread the story of their expedition and the news that Mexico
was independent, trade barriers were relaxed, and the road to Santa Fe was
clear. Other expeditions, Colonel Benjamin Cooper's and William Becknell's,
were already on the way.]

256 Covington, Kenton Co., Ky., on the Ohio opp. Cincinnati.

Bibliography

Part I. Government Documents

Carter, Clarence E., ed. *Territorial Papers of the United States.* 26 vols. Washington, 1932–62.

Hodge, Frederick Webb, ed. *Handbook of American Indians North of Mexico.* Bureau of American Ethnology Bulletin No. 30. 2 parts. Washington: Government Printing Office, 1907, 1910.

Mooney, James. "Calendar History of the Kiowa Indians." In *Seventeenth Annual Report of the Bureau of American Ethnology . . . 1895–96,* part 1, pp. 141–468. 2 parts. Washington: Government Printing Office, 1898.

Part II. Books

Bancroft, Hubert Howe. *History of Arizona and New Mexico, 1530–1888.* San Francisco: History Company, 1889.

———. *History of California.* 6 vols. San Francisco: A. L. Bancroft, 1884–88.

Becknell, William. "Journal of Two Expeditions from Boone's Lick to Santa Fé, by Capt. Thomas Becknell," in *Southwest on the Turquoise Trail: The First Diaries on the Road to Santa Fe,* ed. by Archer Butler Hulbert (Colorado Springs: Stewart Commission of Colorado College and Denver Public Library, 1933), 56–68.

Bowen, Emanuel. *A Complete System of Geography.* 2 vols. London, 1747.

Branch, Edward Douglas. *The Hunting of the Buffalo.* Lincoln: University of Nebraska Press, 1962.

Brower, Jacob V. *Harahey.* St. Paul: H. L. Collins, 1899.

———. *Quivira.* St. Paul: H. L. Collins, 1898.

Brown, Joseph C. "Field Notes of Joseph C. Brown, United States Surveying Expedition," in *Southwest on the Turquoise Trail: The First Diaries on the Road to Santa Fe,* ed. by Archer Butler Hulbert (Colorado

Springs: Stewart Commission of Colorado College and Denver Public Library, 1933), 107–31.

Carter, Harvey L. "Ewing Young." In LeRoy R. Hafen, ed., *Mountain Men and the Fur Trade of the Far West*, II, 379–401. 6 vols. Glendale, Calif.: Arthur H. Clark, 1965–68.

Charlevoix, Pierre F. X. *Histoire et description generale de la Nouvelle France*. 6 vols. Paris, 1744.

Cooke, Philip St. George. *Scenes and Adventures in the Army: Or, a Romance of Military Life*. Philadelphia, 1859.

Favour, Alpheus. *Old Bill Williams, Mountain Man*. Chapel Hill: University of North Carolina Press, 1936.

Ferris, Warren Angus. *Life in the Rocky Mountains, 1830–1835*. Salt Lake City: Rocky Mountain Book Shop, [1940].

Foreman, Grant. *Indians and Pioneers: The Story of the American Southwest Before 1830*. Norman: University of Oklahoma Press, 1936.

———. *Pioneer Days in the Early Southwest*. Cleveland: Arthur H. Clark, 1926.

Fuller, Harlin M., and LeRoy R. Hafen, eds. *The Journal of Captain John R. Bell*. Glendale, Calif.: Arthur H. Clark, 1957.

Gardiner, Dorothy. *West of the River*. New York: Thomas Y. Crowell, 1941.

Garrard, Lewis H. *Wah-To-Yah and the Taos Trail*, ed. by Ralph P. Bieber. Glendale, Calif.: Arthur H. Clark, 1938.

Grant, Blanche C. *When Old Trails Were New: The Story of Taos*. New York: Press of the Pioneers, 1933.

Gregg, Josiah. *Commerce of the Prairies*, ed. by Max L. Moorhead. Norman: University of Oklahoma Press, 1954.

Gregg, Kate L. *The Road to Sante Fe*. Albuquerque: University of New Mexico Press, 1952.

Grinnell, George Bird. *The Fighting Cheyennes*. Norman: University of Oklahoma Press, 1956.

Hafen, LeRoy R. "John D. Albert." In LeRoy R. Hafen, ed., *Mountain Men and the Fur Trade of the Far West*, II, 21–26. 6 vols. Glendale, Calif.: Arthur H. Clark, 1965–68.

Hammond, George P., and Agapito Rey, eds. *Narratives of the Coronado Expedition*. Albuquerque: University of New Mexico Press, 1940.

Hart, Stephen Harding, and Archer Butler Hulbert, eds. *Zebulon Pike's Arkansaw Journal*. [Denver]: Stewart Commission of Colorado College and Denver Public Library, 1932.

Hodge, Frederick Webb. *Journey of Coronado*. San Francisco: Grabhorn Press, 1933.

Hughes, John Taylor. *Doniphan's Expedition*. Cincinnati, 1848.

Hulbert, Archer Butler, ed. *Southwest on the Turquoise Trail: The First Diaries on the Road to Santa Fe.* Colorado Springs: Stewart Commission of Colorado College and Denver Public Library, 1933.

Jackson, Donald, ed. *The Journals of Zebulon Montgomery Pike.* 2 vols. Norman: University of Oklahoma Press, 1966.

James, Edwin, comp. "An Account of an Expedition from Pittsburgh to the Rocky Mountains, performed in the years 1819, 1820." Reprinted in Reuben G. Thwaites, ed., *Early Western Travels, 1748–1846,* vols. XIV–XVII. 32 vols. Cleveland: Arthur H. Clark, 1904–07.

James, Thomas. *Three Years among the Indians and Mexicans,* ed. by Walter B. Douglas. St. Louis: Missouri Historical Society, 1916.

Lavender, David. *Bent's Fort.* Garden City, N.Y.: Doubleday, 1954.

Le Page du Pratz, Antoine Simon. *Histoire de la Louisiane.* 3 vols. Paris, 1758.

Lowie, Robert H. *The Crow Indians.* New York: Farrar and Rinehart, 1935.

Magoffin, Susan Shelby. *Down the Santa Fe Trail and into Mexico,* ed. by Stella M. Drumm. New Haven: Yale University Press, 1962.

Marmaduke, M. M. "Journal," in Archer Butler Hulbert, ed., *Southwest on the Turquoise Trail: The First Diaries on the Road to Santa Fe,* 69–77. Colorado Springs: Stewart Commission of Colorado College and Denver Public Library, 1933.

Mathews, John Joseph. *The Osages: Children of the Middle Waters.* Norman: University of Oklahoma Press, 1961.

Nuttall, Thomas. "A Journal of Travels into the Arkansa Territory, during the Year 1819." Reprinted in Reuben G. Thwaites, ed., *Early Western Travels, 1748–1846,* vol. XIII. 32 vols. Cleveland: Arthur H. Clark, 1904–1907.

Porter, Clyde, and Mae Reed Porter, collectors. *Matt Field on the Santa Fe Trail,* ed., with introduction and notes, by John E. Sunder. Norman: University of Oklahoma Press, 1960.

Richardson, Rupert Norval. *The Comanche Barrier to South Plains Settlement.* Glendale, Calif.: Arthur H. Clark, 1933.

Rolle, Andrew F. "Isaac Slover." In LeRoy R. Hafen, ed., *Mountain Men and the Fur Trade of the Far West,* I, 367–71. 6 vols. Glendale, Calif.: Arthur H. Clark, 1965–68.

Sabin, Edwin Legrand. *Kit Carson Days.* 2 vols. New York: Press of the Pioneers, 1935.

Sanchez, George I. *Forgotten People: A Study of New Mexicans.* Albuquerque: University of New Mexico Press, 1940.

Settle, Raymond W. "Jacob Fowler." In LeRoy R. Hafen, ed., *Mountain Men and the Fur Trade of the Far West,* III, 119–30. 6 vols. Glendale, Calif.: Arthur H. Clark, 1965–68.

Settle, Raymond W. "Nathaniel Miguel Pryor." In *ibid.*, II, 285–88.

———. "Nathaniel Pryor." In *ibid.*, II, 277–84.

Stands In Timber, John, and Margot Liberty. *Cheyenne Memories.* New Haven: Yale University Press, 1967.

Stevens, Harry R. "Hugh Glenn." In LeRoy R. Hafen, ed., *Mountain Men and the Fur Trade of the Far West*, II, 161–74. 6 vols. Glendale, Calif.: Arthur H. Clark, 1965–68.

Stone, Irving. *Men To Match My Mountains.* Garden City, N.Y.: Doubleday, 1956.

Stubbs, Stanley. *Bird's-Eye View of the Pueblos.* Norman: University of Oklahoma Press, 1950.

Tabeau, Pierre. *Narrative of Loisel's Expedition to the Upper Missouri*, ed. by Annie Heloise Abel. Norman: University of Oklahoma Press, 1939.

Thévenot, Melchisedech. *Recueil de voyages de Mr Thevenot.* Paris, 1681.

Thomas, Alfred B. *After Coronado: Spanish Exploration Northeast of New Mexico, 1696–1727.* Norman: University of Oklahoma Press, 1935.

———. *The Plains Indians and New Mexico, 1751–1778.* Albuquerque: University of New Mexico Press, 1940.

Thwaites, Reuben G., ed. *Early Western Travels, 1748–1846.* 32 vols. Cleveland: Arthur H. Clark, 1904–1907.

Tonti, Henri de. *Dernieres Descouvertes dans l'Amerique septentrionale de M. de la Sale.* Paris, 1687.

Wallace, Ernest, and A. Adamson Hoebel. *The Comanches, Lords of the South Plains.* Norman: University of Oklahoma Press, 1952.

Webb, Walter Prescott. *The Great Plains.* Boston: Ginn and Company, 1931.

Weber, David J. "John Rowland." In LeRoy R. Hafen, ed., *Mountain Men and the Fur Trade of the Far West*, IV, 275–81. 6 vols. Glendale, Calif.: Arthur H. Clark, 1965–68.

Young, Otis E. *The First Military Escort on the Santa Fe Trail, 1829.* Glendale, Calif.: Arthur H. Clark, 1952.

Part III. Journal Articles

Barry, Louise, comp. "Kansas before 1854: A Revised Annals," *Kansas Historical Quarterly*, XXVII (1961), 67–93, 201–19, 353–82, 497–543; XXVIII (1962), 25–59.

Bearss, Edwin C. "In Quest of Peace on the Indian Border: The Establishment of Fort Smith," *Arkansas Historical Quarterly*, XXIII (Summer 1964), 123–53.

Bernard, William R. "Westport and the Santa Fe Trade," *Kansas Historical Collections*, IX (1905–1906), 552–65.

[Bloom, Lansing B., ed.] "The Rev. Hiram Walter Read, Baptist Missionary to New Mexico," *New Mexico Historical Review*, XVII (April 1942), 113–47.

Boggs, William M. "A Short Biographical Sketch of Lilburn W. Boggs," *Missouri Historical Review*, IV (January 1910), 106–10.

Chappell, Phil E. "A History of the Missouri River," *Kansas Historical Collections*, IX (1905–1906), 237–316.

Doran, Thomas F. "Kansas Sixty Years Ago," *Kansas Historical Collections*, XV (1919–22), 482–501.

Douglas, Walter B. "Manuel Lisa," *Missouri Historical Collections*, III, No. 3 (1911) 233–68; No. 4 (1911), 367–406.

Dunbar, John B. "The White Man's Foot in Kansas," *Kansas Historical Collections*, X (1907–1908), 54–98.

"Explanation of Map," *Kansas Historical Collections*, IX (1905–1906), 565–78.

Fessler, W. Julian, ed. "Jacob Fowler's Journal: Oklahoma Section," *Chronicles of Oklahoma*, VIII (June 1930), 181–88.

Folmer, Henri. "The Mallet Expedition of 1739 through Nebraska, Kansas and Colorado to Sante Fe," *Colorado Magazine*, XVI (September 1939), 1–13.

Foreman, Carolyn Thomas. "The Bean Family," *Chronicles of Oklahoma*, XXXII (Autumn 1954), 308–25.

———. "William Bradford," *Arkansas Historical Quarterly*, XIII (Winter 1954), 341–51.

Foreman, Grant. "Nathaniel Pryor," *Chronicles of Oklahoma*, VII (June 1929), 152–63.

Gregg, Kate L. "History of Fort Osage," *Missouri Historical Review*, XXXIV (July 1940), 439–88.

Grinnell, George Bird. "Bent's Old Fort and its Builders," *Kansas Historical Collections*, XV (1919–22), 28–91.

Hafen, LeRoy R. "The Bean-Sinclair Party of Rocky Mountain Trappers, 1830–32," *Colorado Magazine*, XXXI (July 1954), 161–71.

Hill, Joseph J. "Ewing Young in the Fur Trade of the Far Southwest, 1822–1834," *Oregon Historical Quarterly*, XXIV (March 1923), 1–35.

"Kansas Historical Markers," *Kansas Historical Quarterly*, X (November 1941), 339–68.

Lowe, Percival G. "Kansas, as Seen in the Indian Territory," *Kansas Historical Collections*, IV (1886–90), 360–66.

Loyola, Sister Mary. "The American Occupation of New Mexico, 1821–1852," *New Mexico Historical Review*, XIV (January 1939), 34–75; XIV (July 1939), 230–86.

McDermott, John Francis. "Isaac McCoy's Second Exploring Trip in 1828," *Kansas Historical Quarterly*, XIII (August 1945), 402–62.

Martin, Bernice. "The Mystery of Paul," *Frontier Times*, XLII (June–July 1968), 23, 42–43.

Martinez, Antonio J. "Apologia of Presbyter Antonio J. Martinez," *New Mexico Historical Review*, III (October 1928), 325–46.

Mead, James R. "The Little Arkansas," *Kansas Historical Collections*, X (1907–1908), 7–14.

Morrison, T. F. "Mission Neosho, the First Kansas Mission," *Kansas Historical Quarterly*, IV (August 1935), 227–34.

Murray, Edward F. "Mountain Men—George Nidever," *Colorado Magazine*, X (May 1933), 93–106.

Root, George A. "Ferries in Kansas. Part IX—Arkansas River," *Kansas Historical Quarterly*, V (February 1936), 22–32.

———, ed. "Extracts from Diary of Captain Lambert Bowman Wolf," *Kansas Historical Quarterly*, I (May 1932), 195–210.

Smith, Alice Strieby. "Through the Eyes of My Father," *Kansas Historical Collections*, XVII (1926–28), 708–18.

"A Survey of Historic Sites and Structures in Kansas," *Kansas Historical Quarterly*, XXIII (Summer 1957), 113–80.

"Union Mission Journal," *American Missionary Register*, II (May 1822), 430–32.

Wagner, Henry R. "New Mexico Spanish Press," *New Mexico Historical Review*, XII (January 1937), 1–40.

Wood, Richard G. "Stephen Harriman Long at Belle Pointe," *Arkansas Historical Quarterly*, XIII (Winter 1954), 338–40.

Wright, Robert M. "Personal Reminiscences of Frontier Life in Southwest Kansas," *Kansas Historical Collections*, VII (1901–1902), 47–83.

Index